The complete paintings of

Cézanne

Introduction by **Ian Dunlop**

Notes and catalogue by **Sandra Orienti**

Harry N. Abrams, Inc. *Publishers* New York

Classics of the World's Great Art

Editor
Paolo Lecaldano

International Advisory Board
Gian Alberto dell'Acqua
André Chastel
Douglas Cooper
Lorenz Eitner
Enrique Lafuente Ferrari
Bruno Molajoli
Carlo L. Ragghianti
Xavier de Salas
David Talbot Rice
Jacques Thuillier
Rudolf Wittkower

*This series of books is
published in Italy by Rizzoli
Editore, in France by Flammarion,
in the United Kingdom by
Weidenfeld and Nicolson,
in the United States by
Harry N. Abrams, Inc.,
in Spain by Editorial Noguer
and in Switzerland by
Kunstkreis*

Translation and introduction
ⓒ Copyright by George
Weidenfeld and Nicolson, 1972
ⓒ Copyright by Rizzoli
Editore, 1970
Library of Congress Catalogue Card
Number 72-2262
ISBN 8109-5526-1
Photoset in England by
BAS Printers Limited, Wallop,
Hampshire

Printed in Italy

Table of contents

Photographic sources

Colour Plates : Carrieri, Milan ; Courtauld Institute, London ;
Held, Ecublens ; Hinz, Basle ; Mandel, Milan ; Nimatallah,
Milan ; Scala, Antella.
Black and white illustrations : Glasgow Museum and Art
Gallery, Glasgow ; Indianapolis Museum of Art, Indianapolis
(Ind.) ; Metropolitan Museum of Art, New York ; Museum
of Fine Arts, Boston (Mass.) ; Národní Galerie, Prague ;
National Gallery of Art, Washington, D.C. ; Rizzoli Archives,
Milan ; Städelsches Kunstinstitut, Frankfurt ; Tate Gallery,
London ; Vallotton, Lausanne.

Introduction

It is perhaps difficult today to appreciate the excitement which Cézanne's work aroused in painters, writers and critics at the turn of the century. He had been struggling at his art for over thirty years and yet people thought of him as a discovery, a new talent and an overlooked master. Gustave Geoffroy, one of the first historians of Impressionism met Cézanne in 1894 and wrote: "All the little known facts about his life, his almost secret productivity, the rare canvases which seem to follow none of the accepted rules of publicity, all these give him a strange renown, already distant; a mystery surrounds his person and his work. Those in search of the unfamiliar, who like to discover things which have not been seen, speak of Cézanne's canvases with a knowing air, giving information like a password."

Even painters who had known Cézanne for most of their working lives were surprised by his work. No one had been closer to him than Pissarro and no one had done more to encourage and help him through the many difficult patches of his career. Yet the first Cézanne exhibition, organised by Vollard in 1895, overwhelmed him and he spoke of Cézanne's "astonishing subtlety, truth and classicism". He was particularly impressed by the large figure paintings, which were in many ways the most difficult to appreciate. "Curiously enough," he wrote to his son, "while I was admiring this strange disconcerting aspect of Cézanne, familiar to me for many years, Renoir arrived. But my enthusiasm was nothing compared to Renoir's. Degas himself is seduced by the charm of this refined savage. Monet, all of us. Are we mistaken? I don't think so."

Younger artists began to seek out his work and in the early 1900s Picasso and Braque saw their first Cézannes. At the Salon d'Automne of 1904 and 1905 Cézanne's contribution made a strong impression and in the winter of 1904 those two remarkable American collectors, Leo and Gertrude Stein, bought their first major Cézanne, a portrait of the artist's wife. Two English critics, Roger Fry and Clive Bell, joined the growing number of admirers and their enthusiasm, expressed through writings and the famous Grafton Gallery exhibition of 1910–11, helped change the course of British art. "Those artists among us whose formation took place before the war," wrote Fry, "recognise Cézanne as their tribal deity . . ."

There is a good reason why Cézanne appealed so strongly to painters in the early years of this century, and continues to do so today: few artists have left such a clear record of the process by which a painting is constructed. Cézanne's method is visibly imbedded into the surface of his canvases. You can see the dabs of paint building up to form the contours and planes of an object. You can sense the picture forming with each mark. According to Vollard, Cézanne used very pliable brushes made of sable or polecat hair. After each touch he washed them in his medium-cup filled with turpentine. Painting, for Cézanne, was a laborious, protracted business. He followed the Impressionist method of working straight onto the canvas, first studying the motif, then looking at the paint on his palette, dipping his brush into the paint and finally applying the dab to the canvas. The difference in Cézanne's case was that each step in this chain of events was a drawn-out effort of will, requiring immense concentration and perseverance. Pictures took months to advance: they could never be said to have been completed. His apples and oranges would rot while he painted them and he was forced to use artificial flowers in some of his still-lifes. His sitters suffered as much as the artist. At any moment he was liable to fly into a tantrum and hack a portrait to pieces. Vollard says that when he sat for his portrait he was careful to avoid all controversial subjects. After 115 sessions Cézanne abruptly abandoned the project saying: "The front of the shirt is not bad."

In the last years of his life Cézanne mellowed and endeavoured to pass on his views about art and painting to young admirers like Charles Camoin and Émile Bernard. Cézanne became the painters' painter, the forerunner of Cubism, the artist who attempted to "redo Poussin after nature" and advised young painters "to treat nature by the cylinder, the sphere, the cone, everything in proper perspective so that each side of an object is directed towards a central point".

There is a dark side to Cézanne, like the dark side to the moon. It is rarely seen and often conveniently forgotten. It is the Romantic, the follower of Delacroix, the student who copied Rubens and Veronese in the Louvre and drew Baroque sculpture, the young man who was anti-classical and anti-Ingres. Cézanne, as has been pointed out, was the first "wild-man of modern art", a precursor of Expressionism. In the 1860s there were many artists who questioned the dominance of the Academy over the art schools and Salons, but Cézanne appeared to be the most bitterly opposed to the system. He transported his canvases to the Salon in a wheelbarrow, works which he knew would be rejected. The polite, well-dressed Manet, who had been rejected himself on more than one occasion, once asked Cézanne what he was intending to send to the forthcoming Salon. "A pot of shit", was the short reply.

Cézanne's explosive temper, his over-sensitivity and suspiciousness were well-known to his friends. His coarse language was matched by an unkempt, dirty appearance. His big black beard, and rugged peasant countenance must have terrified those who did not know him. It was this man who, people said, painted with a "pistol loaded with paint". One work, *A Modern Olympia* (no. 250), reproduced here on the cover, became Cézanne's chief contribution to the first Impressionist exhibition of 1874, where it must have seemed far removed in spirit and technique from the landscapes of the Impressionists. In *A Modern Olympia* and other works of this period, the prematurely balding figure of the artist is seen seated in the foreground. Before him are a series of bleary, overblown, naked females, hideously distorted, who hide their femininity by appearing to crouch or squat on their haunches, or by turning their backs to the spectator and the painter, lying front-down on the grass, their buttocks perched on vast thighs like substitute breasts. The drawing in these paintings is on the level of graffiti, but the colour is strong and sensual. In the last hundred years there have been few works, either by the Expressionists or by a modern painter like Francis Bacon to equal the unrestrained emotionalism of these dark paintings.

Cézanne had something to say, but to his mortification he felt that he had not the means to say it. He lacked the gift of illustration, the sort of talent which any commercial artist can pick up at art school. In vain Zola tried to encourage his former school companion: "One sentence in your letter made a bad impression upon me," he wrote. "It was this: 'Painting which I love, even though I am not successful, etc., etc.' You, not successful, I think you deceive yourself! I have already told you: in the artist there are two men, the poet and the workman. One is born a poet, one becomes a workman. And you, who have the spark, who possess what cannot be acquired, you complain when all you need to succeed is to exercise your fingers, to become a workman!"

Both men agreed that skill alone was not enough to make an artist. In 1866 Zola defined his and Cézanne's belief, explaining, "a work of art is a corner of nature seen through a temperament", and on the title page of a pamphlet reprinting his Salon reviews are the words, "that which I seek above all is a man and not a picture". All who came in contact with Cézanne agreed he had "temperament". His examiner for the École des Beaux-Arts, M. Mottez, explained the reason for his rejection: "Cézanne has the proper temperament for a colourist; unfortunately his work is extreme."

Cézanne never seems to have doubted that he had "temperament", and he used to divide other painters into those who possessed this quality and those who did not: "Manet hits off the right tone – but his work lacks unity – and temperament too", he said to Vollard. And to the painter Guillemet he remarked: "Don't you think your Corot is a little short on temperament?" The painting he admired was "*couillarde*" or "husky", and the rest he considered more or less "emasculated".

It is that very "temperament" which, in a sense, saved Cézanne. He never lapsed into mechanical repetition. Every painting, even if it was based on a motif he had studied a hundred times over, required all his concentration. Every brushstroke was a positive effort; every moment spent before the canvas was a positive affirmation of his "temperament". It is this emotional aspect of Cézanne, the barely concealed rage which lies behind every dab of paint, which supports the Classicist, the painter of spheres, cones, and cylinders, and the forerunner of Cubism.

IAN DUNLOP

An outline of the artist's critical history

The usual documentation, compiled from first-hand knowledge of the man and his development as an artist, is almost entirely lacking as far as Cézanne is concerned. Yet this very dearth turns to a kind of advantage, in that it gives him a charisma all his own.

There are various explanations as to how it happened. First, the nature of the artist himself. His range of sensitivity makes him emerge as a man both proud and despondent, shy and assured. It began in his young days, when the options were open on a literary career too. His preference, in becoming an artist, may be read as an inkling of perennial awareness, and this amounts to so much more than the hint of precocious talent.

As time went by, he was always on the move. Tempestuous moods and feelings drove him from one place to another, each for a little while where he could live and work. This chronic unrest seldom comes across in his paintings, which breathe the same air of search and research, in profound need of perfection. Then there is the difficulty he experienced in making firm friends, after the early period, in itself significant. And again, his generosity in later years when young artists – Camoin and Bernard among them – found a ready welcome at his Provençal home. They wanted his advice, for different motives, either in so many words or direct from his work.

The upshot has been that – apart from some heart-warming declarations of support, like Rivière's now famous piece of 1877, followed by others at irregular intervals – an approach could best be made through Cézanne's letters, and his friends'. In trying to ascertain the course of his artistic and spiritual progress by this means, the first batch concerns his relationship with Zola. It marked a turning-point. In some ways, Zola can be credited with having encouraged Cézanne to go against the wishes of his father. For it was Zola who first saw his possibilities as an artist.

"God help me if I am a bad influence on you, if art and dreaming are not good for you. . . . Come on then, pick up your brushes and make a fresh start. . . . I have faith in you. . . . I think I speak for you, at least I feel able to." (25 June 1860).

Their correspondence over the years is revealing, to a far greater extent than Zola's panegyrics whenever the Impressionists were exhibiting. At the same time it is obvious that what ended the relationship was Zola's inability to understand the precise value of Cézanne's contribution to contemporary art. Indeed, the artist was engaged in conducting unique investigations.

Matters came to a head in 1886, when *L'Oeuvre* was published.

Some of the writer's notes for the book make clear his intentions. The thumb-nail sketch of the leading character, Claude Lantier, reads: "He is a flawed genius, short of fulfilment. Very little is missing, a bit of balance in this direction or that. In addition, he has produced some absolute marvels. A Manet, a Cézanne – dramatised. More of a Cézanne."

Contemporary evidence may therefore be deemed to be of relative value only, and no vital import. It is mostly episodic: Vollard, or Gasquet, or the *Souvenirs* of Bernard. When his work is admired, and this goes for later publications as well, evaluation is seldom properly grounded. The monograph of Fry (1927) is the first to be rigorously appreciative.

Expert opinion since then has gradually begun to delve. Over the last forty to fifty years, progress has been made, especially with regard to the origins of Cubism. But the letters remain a prime source for discerning what the artist was thinking or feeling; his motivations, his ideas, his results are recorded with the same honesty which went into his work.

Cézanne has come in for more abusive treatment – at the hands of both press and public, over the last fifteen years – than any other artist you care to name. Hardly a harsh word that has not been said of him at one time or another. And his reputation, for that matter, is still notorious . . .

What he most closely resembles is a Greek of the golden age. That imperturbable calm, in all of his canvases is also found alike in ancient Greek painting or vases. Those who ridicule his *Bathers*, for example, are just like the Barbarians who find fault with the Parthenon.

Cézanne is a great painter. It has been alleged that he did not know how to draw, by people who have never held crayon or brush. "Not right", they cry, failing to discern so tremendously refined and talented an achievement for what it is.

I am well aware that, all things considered, Cézanne cannot have the success of fashionable painters . . . but his work has the inexpressibly compelling quality of Biblical times or ancient Greece. The movements of his figures are simple but on a grand scale, like statuary; his landscapes are majestic and impressive; his still-lifes fine, and with tonal values so near reality that there is something awesome about them. His painting never fails of impact. This is because of his ability which enables him to endow the canvas with the full force of feeling which nature moves in him. G. RIVIÈRE, in *L'Impressionniste*, 14 April 1877

A revelation as a colourist ... who contributed more than Manet to the Impressionist movement. An artist whose retina is diseased, and his visual perception so far from the normal that he found a new art over the horizon. In these terms may be summarised Cézanne, the all-too-forgotten. J.-K. HUYSMANS, *Certains*, 1889

... and then it suddenly appears that Zola's friend, this mystery man from Provence, a painter full of ideas if not whole, subtle and yet crude, is a great man. A great man? Not a bit of it; more a case of turn and turn about. But undoubtedly a temperament to watch; the new school owes him a good deal, perhaps more than they realise. A. ALEXANDRE, in *Le Figaro*, 9 December 1895

He commits the blunders and errors of a true primitive. G. LECOMTE, in *La Revue d'Art*, 1899

There are a dozen works, landscapes and portraits signed by an ultra-Impressionist named Cézanne, enough to make Brisson merry. It is all very funny, especially the bronzed and bearded head whose cheeks must have been laid on with a trowel and looking mighty eczematous ...

The experts, who are at their wits' end about how to list such vagaries, have simply described each one as: Juvenile Period ...

Had Cézanne been in the nursery when such a sickening mess was made, it would be no laughing matter ... but when the keeper of Médan [Zola] actually supports such folly, what is one to think? ...

Admit Cézanne ... and you might as well set fire to the Louvre ... H. ROCHEFORT, "L'Amour du Laid", in *L'Intransigeant*, 9 March 1903

His Estaque landscapes transform a lovely land of sapphire and gold into a leaden bog where the light never smiles.

The name of Cézanne is going to remain linked with the daftest art of the last fifteen years. C. MAUCLAIR, in *La Revue Bleue*, 21 October 1904

Being a good workman and doing a decent job was for him the key to everything. Good painting meant good living. He gave himself entirely, his whole strength behind each stroke of the brush. You need only have seen him at work, painfully tense, his face as if in prayer, to realise how much spirit went to the task. He was shaking all over. Hesitant, his forehead carked

with unseen thought, chest sunken, shoulders hunched and hands all a-trembling until the moment came. Then firm and fast, they started to work gently and always from right to left, with a will of their own. He would step back a couple of paces, then let his eyes return to the objects. R. M. RILKE, Letter to Clara, 9 October 1907

It was amusing to watch the public at a loss. They had been spoiled for work of such burning sincerity by run-of-the-mill painters who in turn felt themselves outraged. People's values are supposed to have improved but it was like being back in the days of Duret. Visitors to the little Impressionist exhibitions used to laugh out loud on the staircase, before they even set foot inside. Now young people's enthusiasm has more than made up for such silly behaviour. They realise what a boon it is, a self-improving occasion given them this year by Cézanne, and last year by Gauguin. C. MORICE, in *Le Mercure de France*, 1 November 1907

Not to have seen him painting makes it hard to appreciate how slow and burdensome work was to him sometimes. In my portrait, the canvas is bare in two places. I mentioned this to Cézanne. He replied: "If all goes well at the Louvre by-and-by, perhaps tomorrow I shall know what to do about it. Try and understand ... if I fill in anyhow, I shall have to start the picture all over again from that point." A. VOLLARD, *Paul Cézanne*, 1914

He was so entirely unimaginative as to be quite unable to choose those forms most suitable to convey the idea of harmony which he wished to express. He never made choice of one among a large number of objects, in order to present the median element and thus embody all. Instead he would pick any object whatsoever, regardless of whether it was ugly or beautiful, and make his choice from there. The object acquired such unity of character and force of expression that it came across like the law ...

He was a painter. Nothing interested him in reality outside the juxtaposition of colour and form imparted by light and shade to objects. The laws thus revealed were so unsparing that a lofty spirit might take them as governing the life of body or mind. E. FAURE, *P. Cézanne*, 1926

To give Paul Cézanne his true parentage, Michelangelo and Æschylus are names to conjure with. Like the Tuscan, he knew the mystic force which mute objects release, whether rocks or trees. Like the Greek, he sensed the untamed power implicit in the heart of unstudied people. His landscapes and figures are infused with this two-fold strength. It makes his work rough going – as flinty, fierce and fought-over as theirs is – and yet a ground where flower and herbage can lift a modest head with the simplicity and spontaneity of nature.

For Cézanne to contrive to depict material of this solemnity meant cutting through a lot of imaginative undergrowth so that the style alone might convey the sacred drama. Indeed, his colour and drawing are pared down, not to say poor and brutal. In his painting, there recurs the chromatic conflict which Masaccio was the first to evoke with any realism, in the Brancacci chapel of the Carmine church; the vigorous twist and turn are those of Tintoretto.

Unhampered by rule or reservation, his style comes across with the harshness of outline seen in living things, and in surroundings. A. SOFFICI, *Scoperte e massacri*, 1929[2]

The Provençal's great merit was to return painting to a mainstream course. As a result, the art of a whole epoch may be held to stem from his initiative and effort. The Positivist period left a backwash of experiment *a priori* (luminist, divisionist, complementarist). These were all cast aside and the return made to painting nature in the soul's magic looking-glass. The standpoint was no longer emotive or perceptual (as it had been with the Impressionists). Instead, it meant a profound religious commitment on a grand scale. In the light of history, we may call it essentially Italian . . .

Cézanne never paints according to a plan that is more or less revolutionary. He works under pressure; in a mystical way, it directs and devours him. His palette sings or cries, screaming as the drama unfolds. His art has nothing of the hedonist, descriptive or phenomenal. In his canvases, painting as understood by Manet and Monet is outclassed. It is no longer a question of what is "temperamentally true" as Zola saw it. Indeed, there is an ethical and transcendental element in his work, of which Zola's approach contains no inkling. This is the connecting link between Cézanne and the great Italians: Giotto, Masaccio, Michelangelo, Tintoretto, Caravaggio . . .

The spiritual aspect of Cézanne's Italianism is herein comprised, not like Poussin, after the Italian fashion, but in essence. His feeling finds outward expression in a manner, also characteristically Italian.

The crux of his style concerns volume, the interplay of light and shade. The possible variations (intensity, position, thrusting or static) represent his syntax. This is shaped and coloured relative to the degree of chiaroscuro.

It all goes to make him an heir of the Venetians, and of that sculptural tradition founded on the towering personality of

Giotto and the polyhedral mass, and on Masaccio, hewing his figures from great chiaroscuro columns. M. TINTI, "Italianismo di Cézanne", in *Pinacotheca*, March-June 1929

No one in the history of art ever clung to the unchanging more inexorably than Cézanne. The great dream of stability went out with classical thinking, science having contributed instead the idea that everything is always changing. The Impressionist movement accepts this. . . . Cézanne resists. A last flicker of Latinity, trying to recreate the security which went up in smoke in the seventeenth century. With patience and passionate devotion, in search of what is solid and will endure: form and structure, the eternal bases of reality and thought, the outward life and that of the mind. R. HUYGUE, *Cézanne*, 1936

The greatness of Cézanne, contemporary with the Impressionists, their friend and sympathiser, lies in the immediate recognition of his own task as that of going further, using their analytical results for a synthesis on his own account. L. VAUXCELLES, "Cézanne au musée de l'Orangerie", in *Le Monde Illustré*, 9 May 1936

A Latin temperament of an exceptionally stormy nature; tremendous powers of concentration, in many ways prone to extremes and full of contrasts; a prey to unrest, yet a firm believer in prodigious dreams; refined, delicate and careful to the point of shyness; imbued with all the formidable logic of a Kant, yet under severe emotional strain: Cézanne is an exceptional man, in the Romantic and decadent sense of the term. He could have just stopped short of full expression. Instead, he tried for many years to bring his unruly being under firm control. It was a desperate struggle and went deep enough to leave his character permanently scarred. C. L. RAGGHIANTI, *Impressionismo*, 1944

Undoubtedly, there are several Cézannes in Cézanne. Imaginative and practical, sensual and intellectual, the southerner and the mediterranean; one is baroque while the other is classical; one is a lover of reality, instinctive and constantly renewed, a painter who handles material like a sculptor his clay, a pastry-cook his dough, a farmer his plot of land. The other is a great traveller in the realms where all is a phantasy of love and delight. The great Romantics had all made brief excursions into that territory; Nerval and Baudelaire were most familiar with its haunts. One is overjoyed with the look of the world and corresponding artistic creation, another disappointed with nature as something man must impress. The baroque southerner loves movement and effect at its most lyrical. The classical mediterranean type favours style and reserve, the old unchanging order. If ever Racine's words about that cruel war when a man is up against himself, applied to a living person, it is to the painter, Paul Cézanne.   B. DORIVAL, *Cézanne*, 1948

Cézanne is alone, desperately so. He does not make followers. He does not try to conquer or convince. He only wants to express himself. To say what he has to say. It means an effort, a pressure which is inevitably painful. It is a moving sight. Cézanne brings forth in sorrow. His best paintings are serene because they are most meaningful. But they cannot entirely mask the anguish suffered in order to achieve, the patience and persistence of the work; the anguish is never quite gone. For Cézanne knows nothing of the open-heartedness, optimism, cheery sensuality of a Renoir. Cézanne withdraws and concentrates his forces. He cannot abide a lyrical outburst. He does not trust eloquent speech any more than he trusts nature not to lay traps for him, either now or later. Nature he respects and worships, but never expects to find it agreeable. A hard second look is all he can give nature's charms. What he wants to know is just the essential, which lasts.   F. JOURDAIN, *Cézanne*, 1950

It is a superficial judgment that finds subjects of scant interest from the human point of view in the works of Cézanne's last period. Colour and composition lodge an immediate appeal. The old masters treated the most important subjects with the same seriousness Cézanne reserves for the form and tonal values of apples, trees or faces. There is great strength in the way he paints. Minute strokes build up until stillness and movement, consonance and contrast are perfectly balanced. His works express man's best qualities: sensitivity, power to reflect, vigour from strong conviction and integrity.   M. SCHAPIRO, *Cézanne*, 1952

. . . from the artist in him, Cézanne received the impetus to reject any kind of mainstay that was conventional or conformist. In the struggle between man and painter, it was the painter that won. And then the contour-line is broken and begins to stretch out beyond the natural limit of objects. It takes a headlong plunge, then back it comes with too little or too much. . . . The phenomenon has been described as a blunder or a piece of baroque by those whose only discernment is academic. In fact, it corresponds to his ability to penetrate beyond appearances. His aim, to discover the *genuine relationships* of which he was so passionately in search.   M. RAYNAL, *Cézanne*, 1954

. . . In fact, Cézanne was not intent on renouncing Impressionist language for a return to plastic form, obtained by traditional chiaroscuro drawing and modelling. Nor had he in mind, like the Cubists, an integral analysis of the various planes of objects and their simultaneous and abstract surface projection. His declared aim, to "solidify". To subject visual appearances to a

geometric norm. This meant nothing else than a longing to recreate – on the exclusive colour base which the Impressionists with Pissarro foremost amongst them had shown him – a pictorial universe. It would be the result of much thought, each step requiring patient application. To recover, in other words, the simplificatory values of flesh and bones which Monet and his circle had felt bound to reject in favour of expressing the more immediate fluctuating aspects which things wore.   G. A. DELL'ACQUA, *Gli impressionisti francesi*, 1956

He did the same motif countless times over. . . . And he took away anything that was accessory or episodic, in order to reduce it to the bare essentials. Then he gave each element the same emphasis, the most that was evident. His backgrounds come to the fore, making an urgent appeal from between foreground objects, and become inwoven with them. Instead of receding, distant outlines seem to make a move forward and stand out. Foregrounds are usually cut, so that the eye travels straight back, there to focus. . . . Object resemblance and descriptive reproduction are unwanted. A few bare essentials and Cézanne can make a still-life like a primitive dwelling, stone upon stone. There are no plans and no allowance for extras. His figures have the same kind of look, stiff-jointed and above all, motionless. A. M. BRIZIO, *Ottocento-Novecento*, I, 1962[3]

A rare specimen indeed, this sophisticated painter who knew how to preserve purity of feeling. Preconceived systems are not allowed to lend their comfortable support; he wants no help from the old-fashioned armoury of classical perspective, which gives a composition spatial balance *a priori*. He is openly undergoing each experience, as if no man before had ever been through them.   L. BRION-GUERRY, *Cézanne et l'expression de l'espace*, 1966

It would not be possible to trace the line of development of modern art without direct and constant reference made to Cézanne. The teaching of the master from Aix-en-Provence has been of fundamental importance for all that came after. The heritage he left is still with us today. He was no restorer of a classical order, a counterpoise to presumed Impressionist disorder, as has been maintained. How much less was he an abortive genius, unable to realise his great potential, as Zola at one point felt. He belonged to the Impressionists' civilisation, unthinkable without it, but he does more, he makes a personal statement about the world as he sees it. It is a vision born of solitude and a desire to build, which began in close touch with nature but attains a dimension of its own. The style relies on pureness of volume and image, and on vibrant colouring – fantastic and structural.   N. PONENTE, *Cézanne*, 1966

Letters of Cézanne

TO CAMILLE PISSARRO

You are perfectly right, grey is the only colour dominant in nature. But it's fearfully hard to get.
Aix-en-Provence, 23 October 1866

TO HIS MOTHER

I must be working the whole time. Not to have something ready for the gawpers, you understand. People usually value finished work but all it wants is a workman's skill and then it's common and artless. When I try and finish something, it's only to do much better next time and get more meaning. Of course, people do come into the picture at some stage. It makes one's admirers so much more stalwart than just going by the appearance of the thing.
Paris, 26 September 1874

TO AMBROISE VOLLARD

Hard at work and in sight of the Promised Land. I wonder if it will be like it was with the Children of Israel's leader, or will I be allowed to enter?

There is some progress to report. But why so long in coming and so hard won? Is art really a sacred calling with no room except for devotees, who must be of one mind?
Aix-en-Provence, 9 January 1903

TO CHARLES CAMOIN

Couture used to tell his pupils, "Good company is what you need" and "Go to the Louvre". But when you have made the rounds, hurry up and leave the great men to themselves. Get your second wind out there, in touch with nature, instincts and those inner impressions of art we all have.
Aix-en-Provence, 13 September 1903

TO CHARLES CAMOIN

The artist sometimes takes a while to get on terms with the model. You must not let your pet master, whoever he is, be more than a guide. Or else we are imitators. The meaning of nature as you take it and your own good gifts are all you need to be free. Do not let the advice or approach of anybody make you change your own way of feeling. Someone older can be a strong influence. But once you start "feeling", your own reaction will out into the light of day and emerge on top assuredly. That is the best way to go about things. Drawing is only giving form to what you see.

Michelangelo is a maker and Raphael a doer, always. Raphael is great but the model is master. He stops to think and then he is no match at all for that great rival.
Aix-en-Provence, 9 December 1904

TO ROGER MARX

Age and ill-health are catching up with me, before I can make that dream of art I have been pursuing all my life come true ever. But I am indebted to those admirers who somehow got the idea of what I wanted to do, even when I was not quite sure myself how to go about making art that was new. I really don't think you can take over from the past, just add one more link to the chain. What it calls for is a painter's temperament and an artistic ideal, meaning an outlook on nature. Then, with adequate powers of expression to get across to the average viewer, you will have got yourself a decent place in art history.
[Aix-en-Provence] 23 January 1905

TO ÉMILE BERNARD

The main line to follow is just to put down what you see. Never mind your temperament or your ability in respect of nature. And you can forget all about what happened before. This is the way for an artist to express his whole personality, in my view, be it great or small.

I am an old man now, near seventy and "colour awareness" from light gives me an awful lot to think about. I can't seem to cover a canvas or put edges on objects, so difficult and delicate have these matters become to me. It makes the image or painting incomplete. Yet one plane falls on top of another, which is where neo-Impressionism came in. Those outlines done in black are quite mistaken and we must do everything to fight back. The answer lies in consulting nature, that is where to find the means.
Aix-en-Provence, 23 October 1905

TO ÉMILE BERNARD

. . . I do believe I have made some small progress in those studies you last had of me. But it pains me to relate that understanding nature better for purposes of paint and extending the expressive range go hand-in-hand with age and failing strength.

Official exhibitions are so dull because the only procedures on display are those already explored, some to a greater and some to a lesser extent. A bit more character, emotive content and comment would be a good thing.

The Louvre is the ABC where we learn to read. It is not enough to get the sayings of famous forbears off by heart. When the museum is left behind, nature is what concerns us. We have to try and get the spirit of the thing right, then record it each man in his own fashion. Time and thinking work to modify the way in which we see. Thus, we eventually arrive at understanding.
[Aix-en-Provence, 1905], Friday

The paintings in colour

List of plates

PLATE I   LOUIS-AUGUSTE CÉZANNE   London, National Gallery
Whole (168×114 cm.)

PLATE II   SORROW Paris, Louvre
Whole (165×125 cm.)

PLATE III   CUTTING WITH THE MONTAGNE SAINTE-VICTOIRE Munich, Neue Staatsgalerie
Whole (80×129 cm.)

PLATES IV-V   A MODERN OLYMPIA   Paris, Louvre
Whole (46×55 cm.)

PLATE VI   JAR, COFFEE-POT AND FRUIT Paris, Louvre
Whole (63×80 cm.)

PLATE VII   GLASS, CUP AND APPLES
Whole (41.5×55 cm.)

PLATE VIII THE ROBBERS AND THE DONKEY Milan, Civica Galleria d'Arte Moderna
Whole (41×55 cm.)

PLATE IX   SELF-PORTRAIT IN A HAT   Berne, Kunstmuseum
Whole (65×51 cm.)

PLATE X　　　SMALL DELFT VASE　Paris, Louvre
Whole (41×27 cm.)

PLATE XI   MADAME CÉZANNE LEANING ON A TABLE
Whole (61×50 cm.)

THE HOUSE OF THE HANGED MAN AT AUVERS Paris, Louvre
Whole (55×66 cm.)

PLATE XIV MADAME CÉZANNE WITH A FAN Zurich, Bührle Collection
Whole (92.5×73 cm.)

PLATE XV   MADAME CÉZANNE IN A GARDEN Paris, Musées Nationaux
Whole (81×65 cm.)

PLATE XVI   SELF-PORTRAIT Paris, Louvre
Whole (26×15 cm.)

PLATE XVII   FARM-YARD Paris, Louvre
Whole (63×52 cm.)

PLATE XVIII   AUVERS FROM VAL HARMÉ   Zurich, Private collection
Whole (73×92 cm.)

PLATE XIX   POPLARS Paris, Louvre
Whole (65×80 cm.)

PLATES XX-XXI   ROCKS AT L'ESTAQUE São Paulo, Museu de Arte
Whole (73×91 cm.)

PLATE XXII   SMALL BRIDGE Paris, Louvre
Whole (59×72 cm.)

PLATE XXIII   VASE, PLATE, INK-WELL AND FRUIT Paris, Louvre
Whole (61×50 cm.)

PLATE XXIV   MAN SEATED   Basle, Kunstmuseum
Whole (55×46 cm.)

PLATE XXV   FIVE WOMEN (BATHERS)   Basle, Kunstmuseum
Whole (65.5×65.5 cm.)

PLATE XXVI   HOUSE AND FARM AT JAS DE BOUFFAN   Prague, Národní Galerie
Whole (60×73 cm.)

PLATE XXVII   BRIDGE OVER THE MARNE AT CRÉTEIL Moscow, Pushkin Museum
Whole (71×90 cm.)

VESSELS, BASKET AND FRUIT Paris, Louvre
Whole (65×80 cm.)

PLATE XXX   VESSELS, BASKET AND FRUIT Paris, Louvre
Detail (29.5×24 cm.)

PLATE XXXI   ROCKS AND HILLS IN PROVENCE London, Tate Gallery
Whole (65×81 cm.)

PLATE XXXII   WOMAN WITH A COFFEE-POT   Paris, Louvre
Whole (130×97 cm.)

PLATE XXXIII   BELLEVUE HOUSES
Whole (60×73 cm.)

PLATE XXXIV   MAN WITH A PIPE London, Home House Trustees
Whole (73×60 cm.)

PLATE XXXV   TWO CARD-PLAYERS   London, Home House Trustees
Whole (58×69 cm.)

TWO CARD-PLAYERS   Paris, Louvre
Whole (45×57 cm.)

PLATE XXXVIII   TWO CARD-PLAYERS Paris, Louvre
Detail (life size)

PLATE XXXIX   TWO CARD-PLAYERS Paris, Louvre
Detail (life size)

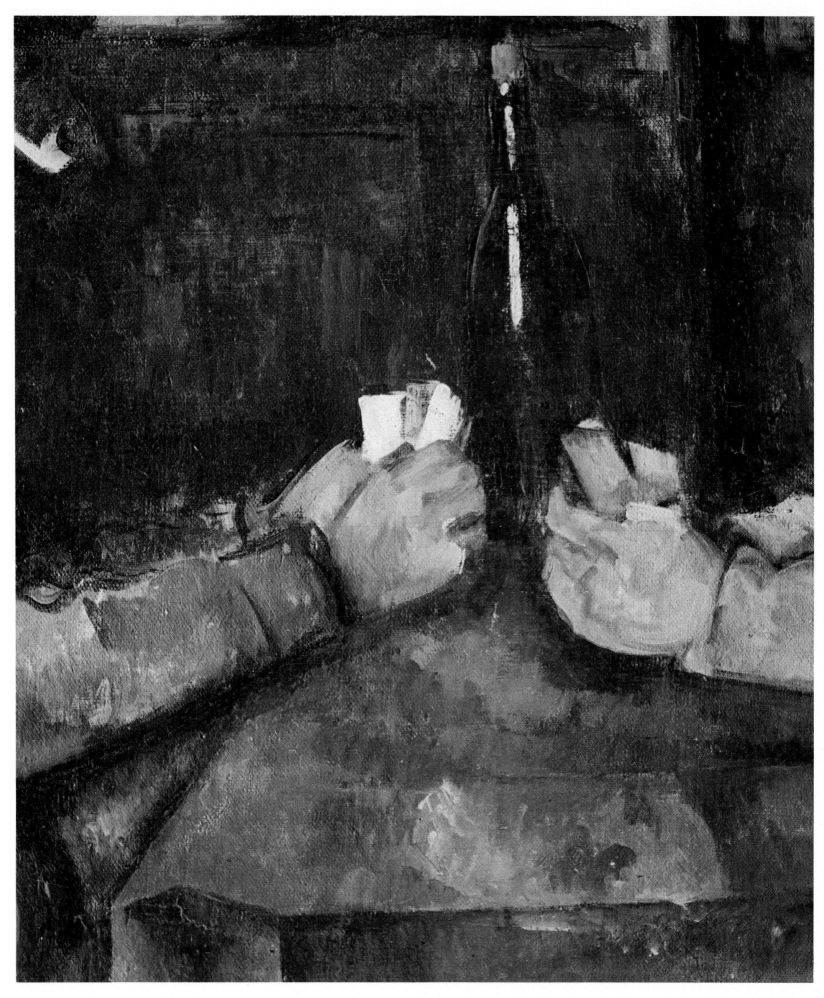

PLATE XL   TWO CARD-PLAYERS Paris, Louvre
Detail (life size)

PLATE XLI   MADAME CÉZANNE IN RED   São Paulo, Museu de Arte
Whole (89×70 cm.)

PLATE XLII   FOUR MEN (BATHERS) Paris, Louvre
Whole (22×33 cm.)

PLATE XLIII   GROUP OF MEN (BATHERS) Paris, Louvre
Whole (60×81 cm.)

PLATES XLIV-XLV

LAKE ANNECY London, Home House Trustees
Whole (64×81.3 cm.)

PLATE XLVI   MADAME CÉZANNE IN A YELLOW CHAIR   Chicago (Ill.), Art Institute
Whole (81×65 cm.)

PLATE XLVIII   ROCKS IN A WOOD Zurich, Kunsthaus
Whole (48.5×59.5 cm.)

PLATE XLVII   THE GREAT PINE São Paulo, Museu de Arte
Whole (84×92 cm.)

PLATE XLIX   BOY IN A RED WAISTCOAT LEANING ON HIS ELBOW   Zurich, Bührle Collection
Whole (79.5×64 cm.)

PLATE L   BOY IN A RED WAISTCOAT LEANING ON HIS ELBOW   Zurich, Bührle Collection
Detail (life size)

PLATE LI   ONIONS, BOTTLE, GLASS AND PLATE Paris, Louvre
Whole (66×81 cm.)

PLATES LII-LIII   CURTAIN, FRUIT BOWL, CARAFE AND PLATE WITH FRUIT   Paris, Louvre
Whole (73×92 cm.)

PLATE LIV   JOACHIM GASQUET   Prague, Národní Galerie
Whole (65×54 cm.)

PLATE LV   GROUP OF WOMEN ("LES GRANDES BAIGNEUSES" - I) Philadelphia (Pa.), Museum of Art
Whole (208×249 cm.)

PLATE LVI   TREES AND ROCKS   New York, Museum of Modern Art
Whole (81×65 cm.)

PLATE LVII   OLD WOMAN WITH A ROSARY   London, National Gallery
Whole (85×65 cm.)

PLATE LVIII   OLD WOMAN WITH A ROSARY London, National Gallery
Detail (life size)

PLATE LIX   TREES AND ROCKS   Paris, Musées Nationaux
Whole (91×66 cm.)

GROUP OF WOMEN ("LES GRANDES BAIGNEUSES" - II) London, National Gallery
Whole (130×195 cm.)

PLATE LXII   PLAIN WITH HOUSES AND TREES (THE MONTAGNE SAINTE-VICTOIRE)   Zurich, Kunsthaus
Whole (65×81 cm.)

PLATE LXIII   VALLIER FULL-LENGTH   London, Tate Gallery
Whole (63×52 cm.)

PLATE LXIV   HOUSE AND TREES Milan, Private collection
Whole (65×81 cm.)

The works

Bibliography

The authority on Cézanne's work remains L. VENTURI. First, his descriptive catalogue (*Cézanne, son art, son oeuvre*, Paris 1936); the material was largely updated by him later. ("Cézanne", *Universal Encyclopaedia of Art*, III, 1958). Venturi was at work on a revised edition of the catalogue (unpublished), with additions, when he died.

On the date order of paintings, some of the exhibition catalogues will be found helpful, namely: J.-E. BLANCHE – P. JAMOT – C. STERLING (Catalogue of the Orangerie exhibition, Paris 1936); G. JEDLICKA (Catalogue of the Zurich Kunsthaus exhibition, 1956); R. WITTKOWER – M. SCHAPIRO – T. REFF (Catalogue of the Knoedler Gallery exhibition of watercolours, New York 1963).

For personal reminiscences, not always to be taken at face value, the following are particularly noteworthy: É. BERNARD ("Souvenirs sur Paul Cézanne", *Mercure de France*, October 1907), although he tends to see Cézanne as the source of his own painting. A. VOLLARD (*Paul Cézanne*, Paris 1914), full of lively information from personal contact with the artist. C. CAMOIN ("Souvenirs sur Paul Cézanne", *L'Amour de l'Art*, January 1921), singing his praises. J. GASQUET (*Paul Cézanne*, Paris 1921), an articulate portrait if not always quite accurate. G. GEOFFROY (*Claude Monet, sa vie, son temps, son oeuvre*, Paris 1924). L. LARGUIER (*Le dimanche avec Paul Cézanne*, Paris 1925) describing his visits when Cézanne was elderly. R. M. RILKE *Lettres sur Cézanne*, Paris 1944). But Cézanne's mind comes out most clearly in his letters, edited for publication by J. REWALD (*Correspondance*, Paris 1937).

The best of the biographies are: G. COQUIOT (*Cézanne*, Paris 1919), G. RIVIÈRE (*Le maître Cézanne*, Paris 1923), G. MACK (*Paul Cézanne*, New York 1935), J. REWALD (*Paul Cézanne, sa vie, son oeuvre, son amitié pour Zola*, Paris 1939), H. PERRUCHOT (*La vie de Cézanne*, Paris 1956). Depicted against the background of contemporary society, by R. W. MURPHY (*The World of Cézanne, 1839–1906*, New York 1968).

A very great deal has been written about his work. In particular, see: J. MEIER-GRAEFE (*Cézanne und sein Kreis*, Munich 1922), R. FRY (*Cézanne, A Study of his Development*, New York 1927), E. FAURE (*Cézanne*, Paris 1936), R. HUYGUE (*Cézanne*, Paris 1936), F. NOVOTNY (*Cézanne und das Ende der wissenschaftlichen Perspektive*, Vienna 1938), A. C. BARNES – V. DE MAZIA (*The Art of Cézanne*, New York 1939), B. DORIVAL (*Cézanne*, Paris 1948), M. SCHAPIRO (*Cézanne*, New York 1952), D. COOPER ("Two Cézanne Exhibitions", *The Burlington Magazine*, 1954), M. RAYNAL (*Cézanne*, Geneva 1954), K. BADT (*Die Kunst Cézannes*, Munich 1956), L. GOWING ("Notes on the Development of Cézanne", *The Burlington Magazine*, 1956), J. RICHARDSON "Cézanne at Aix-en-Provence", *The Burlington Magazine*, 1956), T. REFF "Cézanne and Poussin", *Journal of the Warburg and Courtauld Institutes*, 1960; *The Burlington Magazine*, 1960; *Gazette des Beaux-Arts*, 1960, 1962 & 1963; "Cézanne and Flaubert", *The Art Bulletin*, 1962; *The Art Quarterly*, 1962), B. BARILLI ("Gli impressionisti, Cézanne e alcune teorie della percezione", *Palatina*, 1960), M. WALDFOGEL ("A Problem in Cézanne's Grandes Baigneuses", *The Burlington Magazine*, 1962; *Gazette des Beaux-Arts*, 1965), E. LORAN (*Cézanne's Composition. Analysis of his Form with Diagrams and Photographs of his Motifs*, Los Angeles 1963), S. LICHTENSTEIN ("Cézanne and Delacroix", *The Art Bulletin*, 1964), E. ROSSI ("La prospettiva nella pittura moderna", *Il Veltro*, 1964). More recently, in Italy: N. PONENTE (*Cézanne*, Milan 1966) & M. DE MICHELI (*Cézanne*, Florence 1967) survey the artist's main working problems.

On the watercolours, see especially: L. VENTURI (*Cézanne, Water Colours*, London 1943) & G. SCHMIDT (*Aquarelles de Paul Cézanne*, Basle 1952).

On his drawings: J. REWALD (*Paul Cézanne, Carnets de dessin*, Paris 1951) & A. NEUMEYER (*Cézanne Drawings*, London 1958) also A. CHAPPUIS (*Les dessins de Paul Cézanne au Cabinet des Estampes . . . de Bâle*, Olten-Lausanne 1962).

Outline biography

1839 19 January Paul Cézanne was born at Aix-en-Provence. The address was no 23 rue de l'Opéra. His father, Louis-Auguste, came from a family engaged in business and craft skills; they were originally from Cesana Torinese and the move to France was made in the eighteenth century. His father set up in Aix in 1825 when he opened a hat factory.

Paul was baptised on 22 February in the church of Sainte-Madeleine.

1841 4 July Birth of his sister Marie.

1844 29 January Louis-Auguste married the children's mother. She worked in his factory and was the daughter of a chair-maker; her name was Anne Élisabeth Honorine Aubert.

1844–9 Paul went to the primary school in rue des Épinaux. In 1849, he started at school of Saint-Joseph as a day-boarder.

1848 Louis-Auguste Cézanne took over a bank, the Barges, which was in trouble and founded a new one with his partner Cabanol. It was called, "Cézanne et Cabanoi". The family began to be quite comfortably off.

1852 Paul boarded at the Bourbon college, where he was given a traditional and religious education. He made friends with some of the other boys: Émile Zola and Baptistin Baille.

1854 30 June Birth of his sister Rose.

1856 He attended Gibert's drawing classes at the school of Arts in Aix and became thoroughly versed in the academic style after David.

1858 Cézanne took the second prize for drawing at the school in Aix. He also studied music and played in an orchestra in which Zola played the flute and became a Wagner opera enthusiast. He was often out walking through the countryside round Aix, in the company of Zola and Baille. Then Zola moved to Paris; thus began their correspondence. Cézanne passed the school-leaving examination with a credit in his special subject (literature), and enrolled for a course in law to please his father; but he was already considering whether to become a full-time painter.

1859 Cézanne's father's business flourished. As was the custom thereabouts, Louis-Auguste proceeded to purchase a place a mile or so from Aix. It was called Jas de Bouffan, and had been built originally by a courtier of Louis XIV. Paul spent the summer there, and started a little studio of his own.

1860 His mother and sister Marie lending their support, Paul began to try and persuade his father that he was cut out for the artist's life. He found the work of Loubon, a Provençal painter, interesting and also studied the Aix museum's collection of the Caravaggio school. He made friends with Fortuné Marion who was to become an archaeologist and geologist; also with Numa Coste, the future columnist, the sculptor Philippe Solari, the painter Achille Emperaire and the old painter Villevieille, the journalist Marius Roux, the writer Henri Gasquet and the art critic Anthony Valabrègue.

1861 Parental consent won at last, it was arranged for Paul to go to Paris with his father and sister Marie. As it turned out, he stayed there from April to September only. In Paris he lived in the rue des Feuillantines and attended the Académie Suisse. He met Guillaumin and through him Pissarro and made long visits to the Louvre; he also went to the '61 Salon. He showed some interest in traditional painters such as Cabanel and Meissonier, but the contrast between their work and that of the old masters he found disturbing in the extreme, so he soon lost heart, and neglected his friends including Zola. On his not being accepted for the École des Beaux-Arts, he returned to Aix in September. His first experience of Paris was not a happy one. He agreed to go and work for his father at the bank, but also enrolled for more drawing classes.

1862 Cézanne found work at the bank uncongenial and wrote the following lines on the subject:
"Cézanne le banquier ne voit sans frémir
Derrière son comptoir naître un peintre à venir."
In November he returned to Paris and stayed for a year and a half. Once again, he attended the Académie Suisse. He met Francisco Oller and Guillemet and was often in the company of Guillaumin and Pissarro; also Bazille, Renoir, Sisley and Monet. The Café Guerbois was one of their meeting places.

1863 The year of the Salon des Refusés. Cézanne visited it with Zola. He admired Manet but felt more drawn to Courbet and Delacroix.

1864 Paris found him restless. In July, he returned to Aix. This was to be the pattern from now on; he would live in the north of France and the south by turns.

1865 Publication of Zola's *Confession de Claude*; the book was dedicated to Cézanne and Baille.

1866 At the beginning of the year, Cézanne was in Provence. In July, along with Baille, Solari, Zola, Valabrègue and Chaillou he went to at Bennecourt. (Zola wrote something about this in *L'Oeuvre*.) Cézanne's paintings were still being rejected for the Salons. He wrote the famous letter to the Beaux-Arts inspector Nieuwerkerke, part of which runs as follows: "I cannot accept the judgment of colleagues as legitimate, for I did not ask them to make it." He was introduced to Manet, who admired his still-lifes. In August he returned to Aix.

1867 Cézanne returned to Paris in January but spent the summer at Aix. In October he returned once more to Paris.

1868 Cézanne passed the year mostly at Aix.

1869 Cézanne was in Paris many months but never long at the same address. Meeting with Hortense Fiquet who may have been a model. They lived together without his father's knowledge.

1870 During the war, he was at Aix and in the Marseilles area where he spent six months at the little village of L'Estaque, away from friends and acquaintances.

1871 At the end of the war, he returned to Paris and went to live in rue de Chevreuse, in the same house as his friend Solari.

1872 On 4 January, his son Paul was born. In the spring, he moved to Pontoise with Hortense and the baby. There he set to work with Pissarro and others, painting in the open air, "sur le motif".

In the autumn, the little household was on the move again, this time to Auvers-sur-Oise. Here, he spent the two happiest years of his life in the house of Dr Gachet, one of the few men to think the new art worth something and a collector of work by young artists.

Cézanne also did some engraving with material and equipment provided by Dr Gachet who was interested in the subject. Pissarro wrote to tell Guillemet that he had a painting of Cézanne, "of remarkable power and force".

1873 Cézanne did a lot of view-painting, at Pontoise and Auvers. Met "Père Tanguy" and Van Gogh.

1874 In Paris, at Pissarro's urgent request, he agreed to show at the first Impressionist exhibition in Nadar's former studio. He sent in the *House of the Hanged Man* (no. 136) and *A Modern Olympia* (no. 250), among other works. The comments were scandalised and ironical. Once again, Cézanne was rejected for the Salon.

1875 He met a future friend, supporter and collector, Chocquet. He lived in rue de Vaugirard in Paris but was often away in the south.

1876 Cézanne spent the summer at L'Estaque. After his lack of success in 1874, he declined to take part in the second Impressionist exhibition.

1877 Back at work in Pontoise and Auvers. Eventually he allowed sixteen of his canvases to be hung at the third Impressionist exhibition. But the reaction was unfavourable once more, from both public and critics, with one exception: the young writer, Georges Rivière. Cézanne saw little of his old friends and lived in rue de l'Ouest, Paris.

1878 At L'Estaque, Cézanne painted throughout the year. Every so often he went to Aix, as his mother was ill. He had a serious disagreement with his father who found out about young Paul and resolved to cut his allowance.

1879 Cézanne was at Melun, from May to February of the following year. He often went to Médan, to see Zola who had bought a house there and had begun to write his cycle of novels about the Rougon-Macquart family.

1880 In Paris from February to May of the following year. There he saw more of Chocquet, and also his old Impressionist acquaintances. He met Huysmans and the new advocates of Naturalism. He passed the summer with Zola at Médan.

1881 Cézanne returned to Pontoise, where Pissarro was. Late in the year he spent a while at Aix.

1882 Though he had submitted work for the Salon over a good many years, he had always been rejected. At long last, however, the tables were turned. It came about through the good offices of Guillemet, who presented him as a pupil. Cézanne was in Paris from March to September, then went home to Jas de Bouffan (see **1859**).

1883 He worked for a few weeks with Renoir at La Roche-Guyon. He met Monticelli in Marseilles, and the two of them set off together through Provence. Their favourite rendezvous was Gardanne, from the evidence of the paintings.

1884 In February, Cézanne went to L'Estaque to meet up with Monet and Renoir on their return from Italy. He was often over at Aix.

1885 A brief love affair in the spring left him very low. It was stormy while it lasted and there are some letters written to Zola of this time. He did some more work with Renoir at La Roche-Guyon, then went to Gardanne. In late July he joined Zola at Médan.

1886 Publication of Zola's *L'Oeuvre*. The novel was about a painter called Claude Lantier. Both Manet and Cézanne saw bits of themselves in him. The trouble was that it was a tale of flawed genius ending in suicide and Cézanne found this a harsh judgment on his art from the hand of a friend. So he wrote from Gardanne on 4 April; the letter is not bitter but it is final. He and Zola were long-standing friends but that was all over and they were never to meet again.

On 28 April, he married Hortense Fiquet. His father had eventually met both Hortense and little Paul, but on 23 October, his father died. Paul and his two sisters were left a fortune of two million francs.

Photographs of Cézanne, c. 1860 and 1890.

The artist, from a Pissarro drawing of 1874 and a Renoir pastel of 1880 (see no. 508).

1887 Cézanne was in Aix most of the year and hard at work. He exhibited at Brussels, with the "Groupe des Vingt".

1888 He returned to Paris and took to visiting the Ile-de-France area. He painted at Chantilly and round about, also on the banks of the Marne. He met Van Gogh again and then Gauguin but did not like his work.

1889 Cézanne took part in the Paris World Exhibition, with the *House of the Hanged Man* (no. 136). The rest of the year he spent most of his time at Jas de Bouffan and Renoir was his guest there for a while.

1890 He sent three paintings to the "Groupe des Vingt" in Brussels and visited Paris briefly.

but to painters of the avant-garde and his old cronies he was a master.

Cézanne was in Paris from January to June, then at Aix for the remainder of the year.

1896 He took the waters at Vichy and also stayed at Talloires on lake Annecy. He met an admirer in the poet Joachim Gasquet. He found lodgings in the Paris quarter of Montmartre, where he lived and worked alone.

1897 He rented a small cottage, near Bibémus cave outside Aix and was often at work painting in the locality and the Arc valley.

On 25 October, his mother died. Jas de Bouffan was more painful than he could bear.

1898 Cézanne was at Aix until

1902 Denis persuaded him to show at the Salon des Indépendants. He saw a lot of Gasquet, Léo Larguier and a couple of young painters, Charles Camoin and Émile Bernard, who was later to publish *Souvenirs sur Paul Cézanne*. The Légion d'Honneur for which his name had been put forward by Mirbeau was refused him.

On 29 September Zola died and Cézanne was very upset although they had never met after their friendship ended.

1903 Cézanne spent the whole year at Aix.

1904 At the Salon d'Automne, one room was of works by Cézanne alone. He spent a few weeks in Paris and went, a last time, to Fontainebleau. He sent

deteriorated and they did not arrive in time to see him alive.

He died on 22 October in the house on rue Boulegon and was buried in Aix cemetery.

1907 In October, some 56 works comprised an important retrospective exhibition at the Salon d'Automne.

Granel, now the owner of Jas de Bouffan, offered the Cézanne interiors to the French State. The offer was declined.

1909 Death of Dr Gachet, a friend and collector from the old days in Auvers.

1910 Oils and watercolours, totalling 68 works, were on show at Bernheim-Jeune, Paris.

1911 In the Camondo bequest, the following were acquired by

1928 Cézanne exhibition at Wildenstein, New York.

Caillebotte bequest to the Louvre included four works by Cézanne.

1930 Death of Zola's widow. Some 80 letters from Cézanne were found among the writer's papers.

1933 Exhibition of Cézanne watercolours at Seligmann, New York.

1934 Important Cézanne retrospective at the Philadelphia Museum of Art.

1936 In April, a major Cézanne exhibition opened at the Orangerie in Paris. Another big exhibition in Basle (Kunsthalle).

1937 The Salon des Indépendants shows 85 works by Cézanne. An important Cézanne exhibition also at the Museum of Art in San Francisco (Calif.).

1939 Centenary of the artist's birth. Exhibitions were held in London, Paris, Lyons and New York.

Death of Vollard the collector, friend and agent of the master.

1941 Death of Émile Bernard, painter and author of *Souvenirs sur Paul Cézanne*.

1947 In January, the Galerie de France in Paris ran an exhibition entitled "L'influence de Cézanne, 1908-11".

Exhibition at the Art Museum, Cincinnati (Ohio).

1951 The Gachet heirs gave the Louvre some tokens of the master and three works: the *House of Dr Gachet* (no. 145), *A Modern Olympia* (no. 250) and the *Delft Vase* (no. 216).

1952 Grand Cézanne exhibition at the Art Institute of Chicago, with 127 works; it was later transferred to the Metropolitan Museum in New York.

1953 Brief Cézanne exhibition at Aix, with 24 oils, 26 watercolours and drawings.

From June to September, 23 works of Cézanne are on show at the Orangerie in Paris, as part of an Exhibition on "Monticelli et le Baroque provençal".

1954 The United States embassy in France made a donation to the Academy of Aix, of the Lauves studio where the master once worked.

In Paris, exhibition at the Orangerie entitled "Hommage à Cézanne".

At the Tate Gallery in London, 65 canvases by him were shown.

Further gift from the Gachet estate to the French museums.

1956 Fifty years from the death of Cézanne. Exhibition in Zurich (Kunsthaus), comprising 215 works in oils, watercolours and drawings.

1963 Exhibition of watercolours by Cézanne at the Knoedler Gallery, New York.

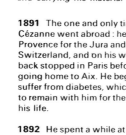

(From the left) The artist sitting in his friend Pissarro's garden, with Pissarro standing in front of him, on the right, 1877; aged about 30 and carrying his material and equipment for working "sur le motif"

(outdoors): portrait of 1894 in his studio, with the Apotheosis of Delacroix *beside him, on which he was apparently engaged (see no. 264).*

1891 The one and only time Cézanne went abroad: he left Provence for the Jura and Switzerland, and on his way back stopped in Paris before going home to Aix. He began to suffer from diabetes, which was to remain with him for the rest of his life.

1892 He spent a while at Fontainebleau.

1894 Cézanne went to Giverny, in order to see Monet. He also met Rodin, Geoffroy and Clemenceau there, but Monet got on his nerves and there were frequent disagreements. At the Duret sale, Monet bought one of his works. There were three more among the Caillebotte bequest which the Louvre declined to accept.

1895 Year of Cézanne's first big one-man show, at the Galerie Vollard in rue Lafitte. He sent in some 150 works, which was too many to display at one time. Public and critics liked him no better than before

the autumn when he went away to Paris.

1899 He sent in three paintings to the Salon des Indépendants. He decided to sell Jas de Bouffan, and took a house in the centre of Aix (no. 23, rue Boulegon) where he lived until his death. It was run by a trusted housekeeper, Madame Brémond. Here he lived very quietly and simply; his wife and son were mostly away in Paris.

1900 Cézanne stayed in Aix, showed at the Paris World Exhibition. A painting by him was bought on behalf of Berlin's Staatliche Museen. Year of Maurice Denis's painting, *Hommage à Cézanne* which was bought by Gide.

1901 Cézanne showed again at the Salon des Indépendants and also at the Salon de la Libre Esthétique in Brussels. He bought some land at Lauves, a few miles outside Aix and had a studio built there.

in some new work to the Salon de la Libre Esthétique in Brussels, but age and his ailment were beginning to affect him and he became harder to get along with.

1905 He showed again at the Salon d'Automne and at the Salon des Indépendants. He at last finished the "*Grandes baigneuses*" (no. 657) on which he had been working for seven years.

1906 Cézanne was represented at the Salon d'Automne with ten works. Denis painted his *Visite à Cézanne*. Friends and well-wishers often called on him but he liked solitude and to consider problems presented by his art.

On 15 October he was out of doors, at work "sur le motif" when he was caught in a sudden squall. He had a seizure and was carried back to the house, unconscious, on a washer-woman's hand-cart. His wife and son were summoned from Paris, but his condition

the Louvre: The *House of the Hanged Man* (no. 136), the *Card-Players* (no. 639) and the *Blue Vase* (no. 493).

1921 Cézanne exhibition at the Kunsthalle in Basle.

In November, exhibition at Cassirer, Berlin. Death of Joachim Gasquet, the author of a book about Cézanne, containing many anecdotes and personal reminiscences.

1923 The Aix municipality named the Chemin des Lauves Avenue Paul Cézanne in his honour.

1926 Important retrospective exhibition at Bernheim-Jeune. It comprised 58 canvases with 99 watercolours.

The "Société Paul Cézanne" founded in Aix.

1927 At Médan in the house of Zola, a painting was discovered: *Paul Alexis Reading a Manuscript to Zola* (see no. 32). Death of the painter Guillaumin.

Cézanne's signature on paintings numbered respectively: nos. 195, 216, 243 and 779.

Catalogue of works

Cézanne's artistic language seems a slow growth when traced through his painting, whatever the level of direct contact and awareness. This is because each cycle of investigation confirmed in the artist that base of experience and performance, on which an inimitable style is built. The formal approach to a space/colour relationship became an experience of epic proportions, explored by the mind's eye "sur le motif", in a way both familiar and constantly new.

Over the formative period, knowledge of contemporary Provençal painting counted a good deal with him. A romantic treatment of landscape painting from life is what the work of Loubon and Monticelli gave him. It was in his youth, when he also enjoyed literary associations which took a lot of living down. His school-days, the friendship with Zola and Baille, the long tramps through the Aix countryside were other landmarks at this first stage of his development. During the early days in Paris, when he was not sure of his own path, visits to the Louvre presented him with the accomplishments of Caravaggio and Velasquez, Zurbaran and Rubens, Tintoretto and Veronese. There were other likely influences among his contemporaries : Daumier perhaps, since he was also Provençal-born; more certainly, Delacroix and Courbet.

Courbet's work may have pointed the connection with real landscape painting and the "feel" of the material. The example of Delacroix was fundamental, not only during the formative period but it may be argued throughout his painting life. For Delacroix – over and beyond questions of treatment and interpretation after the Romantic style – taught him about composition. This, in order to present a wider front, not hide-bound in matters of form, where light and colour might be endowed with their due attributes.

Now it may seem that Cézanne's own nature led him to embark on an emotive and romantic plane. As time went by, a balance gradually emerged between classic formal treatment on the one hand and utter freedom of expression on the other. Classic indeed, but

not at all idealised. Together with the exercise of restraint, these factors produced an outlook whereby he saw nature and depicted it neither by concentrating the spatial vehicles nor assessing the reactions of his retina. It was more a summation by him of what each object stood for. The process was from within ; it was paced by his own reading and the task of restitution.

In the early paintings, up to those datable around 1870, one may discern a headstrong plunge after the reality of objects. The painter tried for his effect by the use of dark outlines, to mark off what objects embodied and denote their position in terms of spatial interrelationship. A romantic sub-stratum, textured by literary references in line with his liking for solitude. The tendency was to dramatise the event, even make it somewhat theatrical in concept. The artist was making a stand, as if involved rather than apart from the event recorded. In the *Black Clock* (no. 126), the formal context already bore direct reference to the life of the objects depicted. Cézanne had begun to wish himself out of the picture.

He sensed the entitlement of painting, in terms of quality, volume, the whole spatial organisation of a work. In this process both of his detachment and of a painting's considered structural entity, he was helped by what he knew of the Impressionists in general and more especially by the company of Pissarro. The components of a work – the *House of the Hanged Man* (no. 136) may serve as an example – no longer vied with each other for the attention of the viewer, according to the predilections of the painter. More of a visual synthesis was achieved here, with light as the guiding feature to determine spatial development planes and call into being the range of living colour.

His quiet work from Pontoise and Auvers strengthened the ground won and indicated the way forward to the days when he was completely self-standing. The ins-and-outs of his dealings with Impressionism, were valuable in helping him learn. For Cézanne, the function

of each brushstroke was less to line it up next to the one before, than to overlap it to some extent, as though under need of constant correction from his perceptiveness. The aim, to make form endure by an uninterrupted process of becoming which operated in reality.

Thus, form and volume tend to take on something of solemnity and density. In works from 1877-88 particularly, a marked structural austerity comes across from the image itself. To speak of the abstract may seem absurd, and out of place with the Aix master's inner evolutive process. It was a crucial period. Cézanne was deeply engrossed in the pursuit of the elusive identity of solids, that is to say their inherent structure. His approach was to strip off the layers of sensory appreciation, one by one. The purpose of this was to distil that moment of impact between artist and quality of subject. The result might be a motif or theme, or food for further thought.

The pattern of choice, in art and letters, is clearer in Cézanne than in a good many other painters. And yet, more can be found out from his life style and his sayings, from those who met him or knew him professionally, than from the study of his work. His reactions can be categorised under two headings. First, with regard to the model, he was shaping and re-shaping in order to get away from blind imitation of reality. Next, with regard to the promptings received from external artistic example.

His use of the colour blue makes the point. He started with the value assigned it by Poussin, whose work he loved. Here, it meant distance and spatial depth. He then absorbed some implications, whether of Goethe's colour theory or the Nietzsche definition of Wagner's *Lohengrin* as "blue music". The colour thus came to have a complicated meaning, mainly on account of the literary streams. It then fed back, in decanting the essences of objects and ended up as a kind of key in balancing other chromatic values. His use of blue was compulsive, not that he was unaware of the mazy ground in which it took its origin. But he gave it a genuine value, an

identity of its own. It was justified and indeed guaranteed within the terms of meaning of a new reality.

Nevertheless, he usually seemed at something of a loss when starting out to tackle a theme. As time passed, there was a gain in exclusivity until the entire working process was characterised, not to say governed, by this means. The series of *Bathers* and *Montagne Sainte-Victoires* show what happened. The artist repeated the theme and it remained stubborn, not fully conveyed and complete. The central motif thus went through many versions. The erotic and sensual early works apart, the corpus may be summarised as : portraits of his wife, still-lifes, landscapes, self-portraits, card-players and bathers. Now the variants are sometimes very slight, scarcely distinguishable, as telling points in narrative or composition. But seen as style, a depth of elaborative detail and consideration lay behind them. Cézanne tried to exhaust the perceptive range. Then the rendering would equate more closely and convincingly with a mind's eye of the thing.

He was always concerned to make his references to nature faithful. This was ensured by analysing a landscape into components, in terms of innate structure. The ascendency of inner awareness over the everyday reality thus produced a synthesis. In the late period, some of the still-lifes seem to exalt objects within a spatial arrangement that responds to the artist's resolute intentions. Chromatic values are concentrated, in an attempt to heal the contradictions attendant upon intuitive grasp that the work is capable of perfection.

The themes may seem few, considering the span of his working life. Cézanne has been faulted for this, on more than one occasion. There is something here, very meaningful for his painting. The language sets out to shed inessentials and try describing reality from the other side. Cézanne's relationship with things and nature may be summed up in this approach to the inner life. His work records the emotional reality, in complex formal structure and unfettered colour.

"My small feeling", he called it. Relative powers of expression were constantly measured. The attitude of mind and spirit was underlined in the kind of precept which the master gave Bernard. It is taken from a letter of 1904 : "Treat nature as cylindriform, spherical or conical, in due perspective." Not that he meant this to be read as a form of extreme geometric faith, or in a categorical way. What he aspired to was a visual order, beyond the physical and objective appearance of reality, and organic to a degree. Indeed, the letter continued : "... for us men, nature is more depth than surface. Whence the need of introducing enough blue tones to let the air into our light vibrations, represented by yellows and reds."

These words almost summarise his painting experience, aimed at rendering form, colour and space in stylistic balance. From the early days through the pro-Impressionist phase to the late period, his artistic language was developing. It spoke of an isolated and autonomous presence. Feeling out of nature remained the vital and irreversible work basis. Skill in handling means of expression was no less indispensable. It required "very long-standing experience". Then and only then could the objective in visual terms and subjective in terms of knowledge meet and mingle.

The master with no school or direct following, the recluse of Aix, yet managed to state the main problems of painting this century and argue a case. After his death, a good many people began to profit by the example. First amongst them, the Cubists. avant-garde splinter movements line up, when placed in chronological order. Picasso's *"Demoiselles d'Avignon"* (1907) came within a year of Cézanne's death. How powerful the example was, may be gauged from Picasso's own words :

"In 1906 the influence of Cézanne, this Harpignies of genius, was everywhere. His art of composition, contrast of form and colour harmony was catching on rapidly. Two problems faced me. I grasped that painting had intrinsic value apart from the life-like representation of things. I wondered whether I ought to give the facts not as seen but rather as they were known."

The date-order of some titles is problematical, for want of precise information. The *Catalogue* therefore follows the arrangement by sub-division of period which was drawn up by Venturi and remains standard procedure. (The Venturi number for each work is preceded by the abbreviation V.).

Within the main groups, succession in kind relies on the known interests of the artist at a given time, and not on some other artificial device. Each group has a heading, which relates to the contents in general or particular. The heading is intended to cover the items so comprised, without further repetition.

The *Catalogue* only concerns oil-paintings on canvas which are safely ascribed. Distinctive symbols may therefore be dispensed with ; where the support differs, a note to that effect has been added. Dimensions (in centimetres) will be found on the line after location, if known ; otherwise, after the title. Wherever the work is signed and dated by the artist, this is entered : (s) & (d). Sometimes, both : (s d).

Location is something of an open question because of works changing hands. Public collections only have been included and private ones where recently verified.

Museum entries, in shortened form for the *Catalogue* purposes, are presented in full in the *Topographical index* at the end of the volume.

Romantic period up to 1871

Cézanne's education was in the French liberal tradition. His friends, his close relationship to Zola – with its personal and literary overtones; the drive to self-expression when the options were still open on other art forms, such as poetry; his first hesitant attempts at painting, with an eye on contemporary Provençal art, especially the work of Loubon: all these crystallised when he went to Paris, first in 1861 and then in 1863.

To point the difference that these two journeys made, two groups under the heading *Various compositions* describe the course of his development. The first, from his school and early student days; the second, more thoughtful and with a touch of the personal element.

Various compositions

I 1859–62
These are basically academic exercises or occasional products (like the screen for his father's study at no. 1 or the Jas de Bouffan interiors at nos 6 to 9). The subjects are mixed and romantic in taste and are taken from famous works (no. 12) and fashion magazines (no. 14) or else are adorned with strange emblems, like The Visitation *(no. 13), where, beside the two women, is a head of Satan, his black hair on end, rising above flames.*

1. Eighteenth-Century Pastoral
402 × 250 1859–60 V.1–3
Screen painted perhaps with a friendly hand from Zola for the study of his father Louis-Auguste Cézanne. On the back are grotesque decorations. It is usually taken as the artist's first work.

2. Girl with a Parrot
23 × 31 1859–60 V.8
See nos 68 and 69.

3. Two Children
55 × 46 1859–60 V.10

4. The Poet's Dream
82 × 66 1859–60 V.11

5. Country Interior with Three Women and a Baby
46 × 38 1859–60 V.9

6. Spring
Paris, Petit Palais
314 × 97 1859–62 V.4
Wall-painting, transferred to canvas, as nos 7 to 9. These were to decorate a room at Jas de Bouffan. The signature "Ingres" on all four and date "1811" on no. 9, are generally taken as an artist's prank (Venturi). Gasquet wrote, "The *Four seasons* make one think of some strange fresco-painter of the fifteenth century working for Épinal . . . the composition is nobly decorative throughout."
About this time or soon after, Cézanne did some more decoration for Jas de Bouffan. They are partly still *in situ*, 1936 (Venturi): nos 12, 16 and 71; partly dispersed: nos 15, 17, 18 and 48.

7. Summer
Paris, Petit Palais
314 × 109 1859–62 V.5
See no. 6.

8. Autumn
Paris, Petit Palais
314 × 104 1859–62 V.6
See no. 6.

9. Winter
Paris, Petit Palais
314 × 104 1859–62 V.7
See no. 6.

10. The Judgment of Paris
15 × 21 1860–1 V.16

11. Chinese Worshipping the Sun
28 × 33 1860–2 V.13

12. Hide-and-Seek
1860–2 V.14
Copy of a noted work by Lancret. See also no. 6.

13. The Visitation
27 × 20 1860–2 V.15
Over the door is written: "Père Zorobabel", in token of the Virgin's ancestry (a man of David's line who led the Remnant back to Jerusalem after the Captivity, 537 BC). Below, in red: "La mère des 7 douleurs – Belzébuth". The head rising from the flames may symbolise the power of evil (Venturi).

14. Interior with Two Ladies and a Girl
Moscow, Museum of Modern Western Art
57 × 92 1860–2 V.24
According to Dorival this was inspired by a plate in the *Magasin pittoresque* or the *Illustrateur des Dames*.

II 1863–71
The two Paris visits of 1861

and 1863 gave Cézanne a double opportunity. First, to study the great masters, old and new at the Louvre. Second, to meet the circle of young painters gathered round Manet after the 1863 Salon des Refusés. His work tends either to echo the masters (e.g. a composition after Caravaggio: no. 26; a stylised El Greco: no. 27) or reflect new thinking. The Orgy (no. 20), a tribute to Delacroix and possibly Couture as well as an obvious influence by the Venetians (Veronese, Tintoretto and Bassano); Geoffroy deemed it a "fundamental point of departure". The subject has been referred (Lichtenstein) to Flaubert's Tentation de Saint Antoine, published in book-form in 1874, though L'Artiste had carried extracts earlier (no. 29 may also refer to it).
The realism of Courbet did not pass unnoticed (see nos 15, 16 20, 29, 30 and 41); Venturi remarked on it as "a corrective to romantic excess".

15. Bather by a Rock
166 × 103 1864–6 V.83
The figure is reminiscent of the *Bather* by Courbet at the Louvre. See also no. 6.

16. Contrasts
1864–6 V.87
See also no. 6.

17. Christ in Limbo
170 × 97 * 1866 * V.84
Probably inspired by a work of Sebastiano del Piombo at the Prado. See also no. 6.

18. Sorrow (Mary Magdalen)
Paris, Louvre
165 × 125 * 1866 * V.86
The subject is religious or symbolical in character, and

1

2

3

4

5

6 7 8 9

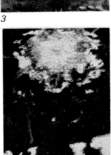

11

10 12

13

14

15   16   17   18 (plate II)   19   20

21   22   23   25

24   26   27   28

29   30   31   32

33   34 (plate VIII)   35   36

there are echoes of Daumier. The dense colour impasto and sweeping brushstrokes heighten the romantic effect, with strong chiaroscuro. See also no. 6, and plate II.

19. The Negro Scipio
São Paulo, Museu de Arte
107 × 83 * 1866 * V.100
The model was a well-known character among the artists of the Académie Suisse. The painting shows the influence of Delacroix (Venturi).

20. The Orgy
130 × 81 1864–8 V.92
This shows the influence of Delacroix (Lichtenstein).

21. Women Dressing
22 × 32 1864–8 V.93
Paper glued on canvas.

22. Nymphs and Satyrs
24·5 × 31 1864–8 V.94

23. Stove in a Studio
42 × 30 s 1865–8 V.64
This is inspired by works on a similar subject of Delacroix and Corot, at the Louvre. It is not a mere copy (Venturi).

24. Two Men out Walking
39 × 31 1865–8 V.96
The two figures are of friends, Marion and Valabrègue.

25. The Abduction
90·5 × 117 s d 1867 V.101
The connection with Delacroix's *Hercules and Antæus* has been noticed (Lichtenstein), male force contrasting with female surrender, the expression of violence and love, the fluent line, the brilliant and rich colour. "In the background, in front of a white cloud, is a mountain vaguely reminiscent of the Montagne Sainte-Victoire" (Rewald).

26. Autopsy (The Laying-Out)
49 × 80 1867–9 V.105

27. Figures Outdoors (Riverside)
27 × 36 1867–70 V.115

28. A Murder
64 × 81 1867–70 V.121

29. The Temptations of St Anthony
Zurich, Bührle Collection
54 × 73 1869 V.103
The theme was repeated some years later (nos 268 and 269).

30. Figures Outdoors (Promenade)
28 × 36 1868–70 V.116

31. "Le déjeuner sur l'herbe"
60 × 81 1869–70 V.107
The theme, after Manet, was also repeated subsequently

(nos 258 and 536). In the foreground, the figure in rear view is perhaps Cézanne.

32. Paul Alexis Reading a Manuscript to Zola
São Paulo, Museu de Arte
131 × 161 1869–70 V.117
Paul Alexis, an admirer of Zola, arrived in Paris in September 1869 ; Zola and Cézanne went south in August 1870, so the work may belong to the interval. Zola could have suggested the double portrait to his painter friend but it was unfinished because of the war. It is set in the garden of Zola's Paris house, rue de la Condamine. It was found in an attic of the Médan house by Zola's wife after his death, and assigned to Cézanne (Venturi).

33. Zola Reading
52 × 56 1869–70 V.118
The writer's visitor may be

Paul Alexis (see no. 32).

34. The Robbers and the Donkey
Milan, Civica Galleria d'Arte Moderna (Grassi Bequest)
41 × 55 1869–70 V.108
The theme, out of the *Metamorphoses* of Apuleius, was used also by Decamps and Daumier among others. The atmosphere is dramatic, indicative of the grandeur to follow later.
See plate VIII.

35. Idyll (Don Quixote on the Barbary Coast)
65 × 81 d 1870 V.104
The man in the centre, in black, may be the artist himself.

36. A Modern Olympia
56 × 55 1870 V.106
The subject was repeated some years later (see no. 250). The title echoes Manet.

37

38

39

40

41

42

43

44

45

46

37. Two Ladies Outdoors (Promenade)
58 × 46* 1870 * V.119
This was taken from a fashion plate ; the two ladies are the painter's sisters : Marie on the left and Rose on the right.

38. Bathers
Christie's sale 14.4.70
20 × 40* 1870 * V.113

39. Female Nude Drying her Hair
29 × 13 1869–71 V.114

40. Girl at the Piano
Moscow, Museum of Modern Western Art
57 × 92 1869–71 V.90
This may be a portrait of the painter's sister Marie.

41. Two Ladies and Two Gentlemen Outdoors (Conversation Piece)
92 × 73 1870–1 V.120
After a fashion plate. This features the painter's sisters Rose and Marie, and his two friends Valabrègue and Marion.

42. Two Bathers and a Fisherman
14 × 21 1870–1 V.1520 A

43. Afternoon in Naples (Rum Punch)
14 × 24 1870–2 V.112
See no. 251.

44. Woman Strangled
31 × 25 1870–2 V.123

45. The Boat of Dante
25 × 33 1870–3 V.125
This is a copy of the Delacroix's painting at the Louvre which was in turn inspired by Dante's *Inferno*, Canto VIII.

46. Hamlet and Horatio
35 × 30 1870–3
First published 1956 (Venturi), this belonged to Dr Gachet. The subject is taken from the Delacroix painting at the Louvre.

Portraits

Compared with the above compositions, this group has perhaps more unity – Cézanne is on the road to a personal style, with an eye to Daumier (no. 48) and more to Courbet (nos 53, 67 and 70). Some are still romantic in concept though the technique was being revised. A third dimension is conveyed by the thick impasto, laid on not by brush but formed with a spatula "which makes the colour more intense and conveys some idea of volume although the painter does not adopt contrasting light and indeed no chiaroscuro to give the relief effect" (Venturi).

47. Self-Portrait
44 × 37 1858–61 V.18

48. Louis-Auguste Cézanne
London, National Gallery
168 × 114 1860–3 V.25
In all probability, this portrait of Cézanne's father was painted at Jas de Bouffan, with a good deal of regard for the work of Daumier. Gasquet wrote of it, that "he [Cézanne] painted it in impasto, large, solid and full-bodied as if he wanted good colours to celebrate the tie of parentage".
See also no. 6, and plate I.

49. Man with a Dark Beard
35 × 27 1860–3 V.20

50. Émile Zola
26 × 21 1861–2 V.19

51. Head of an Old Man
Paris, Louvre
51 × 48 1860–5 V.17

52. Self-Portrait
Christie's sale 28.6.68
44 × 32 1862–4 V.1509

53. Study of a Woman
46 × 38 s d 1864 V.22
Thought to be Zola's wife (Adhémar).

54. Bust of a Young Man
60 × 54 *1864* V.95

55. "L'Oncle Dominique"
46 × 33 *1865* V.75
Probably the painter's uncle on his mother's side.

56. Man in a Cotton Cap ("L'Oncle Dominique" ; Self-Portrait ?)
New York, Museum of Modern Art
84 × 64 *1865* V.73

57. "L'Oncle Dominique"
39 × 30·5 *1865* V.80

58. "L'Oncle Dominique"
44 × 37 *1865* V.82

59. "L'Oncle Dominique" (The Advocate)
63 × 52 *1865* V.74

60. "L'Oncle Dominique"
46 × 38 *1865* V.79

61. "L'Oncle Dominique"
41 × 33 *1865* V.76

62. "L'Oncle Dominique"
40·5 × 31·5 *1865* V.77

63. Dominican Monk ("L'Oncle Dominique")
New York, Haupt Collection
65 × 54 *1865* V.72
One of the best-known "Oncle Dominique" portraits. Again the painting is fiercely executed, the colour applied sometimes with brush and sometimes with spatula. A distant Gothic inspiration, and the white habit of the Dominican order may identify the uncle's name (Schapiro). Lacordaire had been influential in reshaping the Dominican Order ; he had organised a society to encourage religious art which interested the Romantics. This is not a portrait properly speaking (Schapiro) but a mask and symbolic image ; it is expressive of a strong personality, with feelings restrained by the religious habit.

64. Self-Portrait
Moscow, Museum of Modern Western Art
45 × 41 s 1865–6 V.81

65. Anthony Valabrègue
New York, Wildenstein Collection
116 × 98 s 1866 ? V.126
Probably the portrait mentioned by Valabrègue in a letter to Zola, of November 1866 (nos 78 and 79, usually taken as of some years later). "Paul made me sit yesterday for a study of the head. . . . I look so vigorous that it reminds me of the curate of Champfleury's statue. . . . Luckily, it was only one day. His uncle ["Oncle Dominique", see nos 55 to 63] is mostly the model. A portrait comes up of an afternoon and Guillemet makes awful jokes about it." (See details on Valabrègue, in *Outline biography*, **1860**.)

66. Bust of a Man
Winterthur, Reinhart Collection
81 × 62 *1866* V.102
This may be "Oncle Dominique" again.

67. Louis-Auguste Cézanne

200 × 120 1866 ? V.91
The artist's father is reading *L'Évènement*, the paper which printed Zola's article about the 1866 Salon which contained a violent attack on Meissonier, Cabanel and other painters of fashion. The title, clear enough to be read, is a tribute to the writer. The painting shows some considerable development on the formal plane, remarked on by Guillemet in a letter to Zola (autumn, 1866).
On the wall in the background is the still-life no. 124.

68. Girl with a Parrot
28 × 20 1864–8 V.99

69. Girl with a Parrot
45 × 37 ? V.98

70. Self-Portrait with Long Hair
41 × 32 1865–8 V.23

71. Achille Emperaire
42 × 40 1864–9 V.85
See also no. 6, and *Outline biography*, **1860**.

72. Achille Emperaire
200 × 122 s 1867 V.88
The sitter's name is written at the top in capitals. The high-backed chair of floral design is also in no. 67 ; the two works presumably date from about the same time, also on grounds of stylistic affinity. Gasquet describes it as "consumed with hunger for life, a creature of caricature, limp hands and fine, sad face turned aside . . . overhead, his name rather wryly proclaimed, notice-board size : Achille Emperaire".

73. Marie Cézanne
50 × 39 1865–7 V.78

74. Marie Cézanne
St Louis (Mo.), City Art Museum
55 × 38 1867–9 V.89

75. Head of a Man
41 × 33 *1869* V.110

76. Bust of a Boy
58 × 50 1868–70 V.109

77. Young Man with a Dark Beard
1868–70 V.97

78. Anthony Valabrègue
60 × 50 *1870* V.127
See also no. 65.

79. Anthony Valabrègue
1870 V.128
See also no. 65.

80. Man with a Straw Hat (Boyer)
New York, Metropolitan Museum of Art
55 × 39 s 1870–1 V.131
The sitter was a childhood friend of the painter, a notary of Eyguières in later life.

81. Boyer
1870–1 V.130

82. Boyer
Ottawa, National Gallery of Canada
47 × 38 1870–1 V.132

83. Fortuné Marion
43 × 33 1870–1 V.129
See *Outline biography*, **1860**.

47

48 (plate I)

49

50

51

52

53

54

55

56

57

58

59

60

61

62

63

64

65

66

67

68

69

70

71

72

73

74

75

76

77

78

79

80

81

82

83

84

85

86

87

88

89

90

91

92

93

94

95

96

97

99

101

98

100

102

103

104

105

106

107

108

109

110

111

Landscapes

Admiration for Corot is evident in some of the early and delightfully luminous pieces (nos 86 and 88), but Cézanne's interest soon turned to the Provençal painters especially Loubon who was represented at the Aix museum and Monticelli (nos 102, 108, 109), who became a friend and had belonged to the group led by Loubon. To these sources may be attributed the heady colour contrasts; the heightened tonal effect was his own (nos 87, 92–6, 105–6 and 109). About 1870 and only then (no. 107), the treatment of form begins to simplify towards the landscapes characteristic of his prime.

84. Trees and Houses (Romantic Landscape)
26 × 33 1858–60 V.26
  Perhaps inspired by a print

85. Trees and Houses (Romantic Landscape)
26 × 33 1858–60 V.28

86. Path among the Trees
35 × 30 1860–5 V.29

87. Farm-Yard
Parke-Bernet sale 12.2.68
26 × 33 1860–5 V.31

88. Hills with Trees and a Dwelling
19 × 30 1860–5 V.32

89. Woodland Scene
35 × 22 *1864* V.27

90. Woodland Scene
23 × 30 *1864* V.30

91. Hill with Trees and River
22 × 28 *1864* V.1510

92. River in Trees
1865–7 V.33

93. River Bend among Rocks and Trees
33 × 41 1865–7 V.34

94. House in a Clearing
26 × 39 1865–7 V.35

95. Hills with Trees
1865–7 V.37

96. Path by Trees, and a Dwelling
24 × 38 1865–7 V.36

97. Avenue at Jas de Bouffan
1865–7 V.38
  His father bought the property in 1859. The house and farm dated from the previous century and had been the home of a governor of Provence. Local people thought the gesture showy, typical of a self-made man. "Jas de Bouffan" means a windy place. Cézanne loved it and did a great deal of painting there during his frequent long stays.

98. Stream among Trees
35 × 116 1865–7 V.46

99. Boulders
22 × 32 1865–70 V.1512

100. River on a Plain
Lausanne, Vallotton Collection
26·7 × 34·7 1866–8 V.41

112

113

114

115 (plate III)

116

117

101. Village Church
Cambridge, Fitzwilliam Museum
64·8 × 54 1866–8 V.49

102. Clearing
1867–9 V.43

103. Rue des Saules, Montmartre
32 × 41 1867–9 V.45

104. Road
33 × 46 1867–9 V.44
  Described as a view of the Tour du Télégraphe, Montmartre (Venturi).

105. Winding Road in Provence
Montreal, Museum of Fine Arts
91 × 71 1867–70 V.53

106. Cutting
19 × 33 1867–70 V.42
  Scene near Jas de Bouffan.

107. Road with Houses in Provence
59 × 78 1867–70 V.54

108. Garden at Jas de Bouffan
23·5 × 30 1867–70 V.39

109. Pool at Jas de Bouffan
46 × 53 1867–70 V.40
  The pool was in the grounds of the Cézannes' home in the country; the painter reproduced the subject on several occasions.

110. Avenue at Jas de Bouffan
36 × 44 1869 V.47

111. L'Estaque under Snow
Zurich, Bührle Collection
73 × 92 *1870* V.51

112. Fishing Village at L'Estaque
42 × 55 *1870* V.55

113. Sunset at L'Estaque
44 × 60 *1870* V.57

114. Works by the Montagne Sainte-Victoire
41 × 55 *1870* V.58

115. Cutting with the Montagne Sainte-Victoire
Munich, Neue Staatsgalerie
80 × 129* 1870* V.50
  The head of Sainte-Victoire is in the background. This was a motif especially dear to the artist in his prime. See plate III.

116. Fork in a Road
New York, Museum of Modern Art
57 × 70 1871–2 V.52

117. Beside the Seine at Bercy ("La halle au vin")
73 × 92 1871–2 V.56
  Painted from the window of the artist's house in Paris.

Still-lifes

In this line of painting as in landscapes, the artist was to make great strides forward later on. Note the oblique-angled knife, inspired by Manet, evoking a new spatial plane (nos 119 and 129), another subsequently-recurrent feature.

118. Peaches on a Plate
18 × 24 1860–4 V.12
  Deemed a copy of an item in the Aix museum, attributed to Cuyp or an unknown artist of the late eighteenth century.

119. Jug, Bread, Eggs and Glass
Cincinnati (Ohio), Art Museum
59·2 × 76·2 s d 1865 V.59

120. Glass, Pan and Two Fowl
32 × 40 s 1864–6 V.60

121. Bottle, Glass and Lemons
1864–6 V.63

122. Skull and Carafe
60 × 50 1865–6 V.68
  The theme of the skull, treated at this period, later recurs to heightened effect.
  A "sombre canvas of impasto warmly-felt and moving as a Rembrandt" (Gasquet). The

same writer recalled hearing Cézanne recite one evening by the river Arc, the following lines from Verlaine:
"Car dans ce monde léthargique
Toujours en proie aux vieux
      remords
Le seul rire encore logique
Est celui des têtes de morts."

123. Skull, Candlestick and Book
47·5 × 62·5 1865–7 V.61
  See also no. 67.

124. Mug, Sugar-Bowl and Pears
30 × 41 1865–7 V.62

125. Bread and Leg of Lamb
Zurich, Kunsthaus
27 × 35 1865–7 V.65
  The same subject was treated by Claude Monet – perhaps over the same years.

126. Black Clock
Paris, Niarchos Collection
54 × 73 1869–70 V.69

127. Apples and Leaves
1870–2 V.66

128. Relief, Scroll and Ink-Well
Paris, Louvre
1870–2 V.67
  The relief may portray Dr Gachet, done by Solari who

118

119

120

121

122

123

124

125

126

127

128

129(plate VI)

130

169. Pool at Jas de Bouffan
1875–6 V.167
As in the next item, no. 170, the statue of a dolphin is shown.

170. Pool at Jas de Bouffan
58 × 71 1875–6 V.166

171. View in Paris (Roofs)
58 × 72 1874–7 V.175

172. Sea at L'Estaque
New York, Bernhard Collection
42 × 59 s 1876 V.168
View of the gulf of Marseilles; in the background, Frioul islands. Cézanne wrote in a letter of 2 July 1876 to Pissarro: "It's like a playing card, red roofs on blue sea. The sun so fierce that objects rise up in outline, not just black and white, but blue, red, brown and violet. I may be mistaken, but this seems the model's furthest pole."

173. Trinitarian Monastery at Pontoise (The Retreat)
Moscow, Museum of Modern Western Art
58 × 71 1875–7 V.172

174. Trees and Houses
Zurich, Bührle Collection
58 × 47·5 1875–7 V.169

175. Village in Northern France
60 × 50 s 1875–7 V.171
Perhaps a view of Auvers

176. The Côte des Boeufs at Pontoise
65 × 54 1875–7 V.173

177. The Étang des Soeurs at Osny
London, Home House Trustees
57 × 71 1875–7 V.174

178. Trinitarian Monastery at Pontoise (The Retreat)
44 × 54 1875–7 V.176

179. Winding Road
48 × 59 1875–7 V.177

180. Winding Street in Auvers
60 × 73 1875–7 V.178

181. Bed of Torrent from the Pontoise Retreat
Leningrad, Hermitage
50 × 61 *1877* V.170

182. Houses (Roofs)

was to make a bust of Cézanne (1904).

129. Jar, Coffee-Pot and Fruit (Still-Life in Black-and-White)
Paris, Louvre
63 × 80 1870–2 V.70
A tribute to Manet, in composition and treatment of light. The ground and table are in shades of grey. The pot stands out against the white cloth. See plate VI.

130. Vase, Bottle, Cups and Fruit
Berlin, Nationalgalerie
64 × 80 1871–2 V.71

Impressionist period 1872–7

This important stage in Cézanne's development is marked by his sojourn at Auvers-sur-Oise from 1872 and working contact with Pissarro over at Pontoise. The constructive element is stressed, and this has a counter-part in the art of Pissarro who "unlike others, gave Impressionism a wish to build bigger; this required a structural approach to light itself" (Venturi).

Landscapes

Pissarro's influence is here most active in Cézanne's objective tackling of nature, his study of structure and colours where his personality and technique apply a visual filter. The two men often worked together, sometimes on the same landscape (nos 176 and 181); there is also a Cézanne copy of a Pissarro (no. 134). By slow degrees, the artist thus used light and vibrant colour to "synthesise space and volume... which is what gives things a sense of the eternal" (Venturi). The colour impasto is drier and this makes variegated surfaces which reflect light.

131. Water-Mill
41 × 54 1871–2 V.48

132. Mill
38 × 46 1871–2 V.136

133. Garden Wall
22 × 31 1871–2 V.1513

134. Louveciennes
73 × 92 *1872* V.153
Copy of a Pissarro (1871)

135. Farm-Yard
46 × 38 1871–3 V.1511

136. The House of the Hanged Man at Auvers
Paris, Louvre
55 × 66 s 1872–3 V.133
A clear instance of the artist's new style, which has been described as a "process of solidification" (Gowing). "Space becomes compact rather than shapeless, despite the thick paint material; body is given to mass, rather than weight. Fineness of landscape results" (Venturi). Cézanne "takes from Impressionism all he needs to surpass the concept of motionless reality" (Ponente). The painting was shown at the first Impressionist exhibition (April 1874) and regarded as highly controversial. Leroy's contribution to *Charivari*, 25 April 1874, gives a sample of the current reaction. See plates XII-XIII.

137. Woodland Scene
46 × 55 1872–3 V.155

138. Cottages at Auvers
46 × 38 1872–3 V.135

139. Street in Auvers
s 1872–3 V.134

140. Street in the Snow
38 × 46 1872–3 V.137
Probably a wintry scene at Auvers.

141. House and Tree at Auvers
San Francisco (Calif.), Palace of the Legion of Honor (Goetz Bequest)
66 × 55 s 1872–3 V.142

142. House of Père Lacroix at Auvers
Washington, D.C., National Gallery of Art
61 × 51 s d 1873 V.138

143. Dwelling in Trees at Auvers
Parke-Bernet sale 17.4.69
69 × 49 s d 1873 V.139

144. House of Dr Gachet at Auvers
62 × 52 1873 V.144
See *Outline biography*, 1872.

145. House of Dr Gachet at Auvers
Paris, Louvre
46 × 37·5 1873 V.145

146. House of Dr Gachet at Auvers
56 × 46 1873–4 V.146

147. Dwellings at Auvers
Cambridge (Mass.), Fogg Art Museum
40 × 54 s 1873–4 V.156
View from Val-Harmé.

148. The Four District at Auvers
47 × 51·5 1873–4 V.157

149. Street in Auvers
Ottawa, National Gallery of Canada
55 × 46 1873–4 V.147

150. Winding Road in Trees
Chicago (Ill.), Brewster Collection
55 × 46 1873–5 V.140

151. Track with Trees and Houses
38 × 46 1873–5 V.141

152. House among Trees near Pontoise
60 × 73 1873–5 V.143

153. House among Trees at Auvers
92 × 73 1873–5 V.148

154. View of Auvers, with Paling
New York, Ittleson Collection
44·5 × 34·5 s 1873–5 V.149

155. View of Auvers, from Above
Chicago (Ill.), Art Institute
65 × 81 1873–5 V.150

156. View of Auvers through Trees
48 × 58 1873–5 V.151

157. Valley of the Oise
San Francisco (Calif.), Palace of the Legion of Honor

(Goetz Bequest)
72 × 91 1873–5 V.152

158. Houses and Trees on Hillside
1873–7 V.154

159. Boundary Wall
50 × 65 s 1875–6 V.158

160. Pine Tree at L'Estaque
Paris, Musées Nationaux (Walter-Guillaume Bequest)
72 × 58 1875–6 V.163

161. Trees and Village
65 × 46 1875–6 V.165

162. Woodland Scene
54 × 65 1875–6 V.1525

163. Meadow and Trees near Jas de Bouffan
Christie's sale 28 June 1968
39 × 54 1875–6 V.159

164. View at Jas de Bouffan
45 × 59 1875–6 V.1516

165. Trees at Jas de Bouffan
54 × 73 1875–6 V.161

166. Boundary Wall and Trees at Jas de Bouffan
46 × 55 1875–6 V.162

167. Pool at Jas de Bouffan
46 × 55 1875–6 V.160

168. Pool at Jas de Bouffan
52·5 × 56 1875–6 ? V.164

131

135

132

138

133

134

136 (plates XII-XIII)

137

139

140

141

142

143

144

145

146

147

148

149

150

151

152

153

154

155

156

157

160

158

159

162

163

161

164

165

166

93

Berne, Hahnloser Collection
47 × 59 *1877* V.1515

Still-lifes

Unlike the path followed by the Impressionists of the time, Cézanne's investigations of light made him esteem form rather than try to "empty" it. There are a lot of flower paintings at this period (nos 213–25), of near body-like consistency. The knife motif re-echoes Manet (nos 183, 196 and 212).

Fruit and objects

183. Jug, Glass, Knife and Fruit
60 × 73 1873 V.185
Painted in the house of Dr Gachet at Auvers.

184. Bowl with Apples and Pears
25 × 39 1873–4 V.194

185. Faïence Ware and Fruit
Parke-Bernet sale 3 April 1968
40 × 53.5 1873–4 V.189

186. Glass, Cup and Apples
41.5 × 55 1873–7 V.186
See plate VII.

187. Glass, Cup and Apples
33 × 46 1873–7 V.187

188. Glass, Cup and Fruit
38 × 46 1873–7 V.188

189. Apples
19 × 27 1873–7 V.190

190. Apples
Parke-Bernet sale 26 October 1967
12 × 26 1873–7 V.191

191. Apples
Lausanne, Musée Cantonal des Beaux-Arts
16.5 × 23.5 1873–7 V.195

192. Overturned Fruit Basket
Glasgow, Art Gallery and Museum
16 × 32 1873–7 V.211

193. Plate of Grapes and Peach
16.5 × 29 1873–7 V.192

194. Plate of Apricots and Cherries
16 × 22 1873–7 V.193

195. Dish of Apples and Dessert
46 × 55 s 1873–7 V.196

196. Bottle, Glass, Fruit and Dessert (Dessert)
Philadelphia (Pa.), Museum of Art

60 × 73 s 1873–7 V.197

197. Vessels and Lemon
21.5 × 43.5 1873–7 V.221

198. Vessels and Lemon
19 × 30 1873–7 V.219

199. Jug and Cup
Tokyo, Ishibashi Collection
20.5 × 18.5 1873–7 V.220

200. Two Apples and a Half
Merion (Pa.), Barnes Foundation
16.5 × 10 1873–7 V.202
This may be part of a work (Venturi).

201. Three Pears
20.5 × 26 1873–7 V.201

202. Plate of Apples, Orange and Lemon
22 × 33 1873–7 V.204

203. Plate of Four Apples
15 × 31 1873–7 V.205

204. Plate of Fruit
24 × 35 1873–7 V.206

205. Receptacles, Fruit and Biscuits on a Sideboard
Budapest, Szépmüvészeti Múzeum
75 × 81 1873–7 V.208
"Here, reality is on the side of the painter. His own blue, laid on like wadding, his red, his green unshadowed and the reddish black of his bottles of wine" (Rilke to Clara, 1907).

206. Plate of Apples and Sugar Bowl
Philadelphia (Pa.), Annenberg Collection
46 × 55 s 1873–7 V.207

207. Bronze Vase and Sugar-Bowl
27.5 × 51 1875–6 ? V.200
Analogous composition in the centre of no. 625.

208. Biscuits and Fruit-Bowl
53 × 63 *1877* V.209
The hanging in the background, olive yellow with blue flowers, appears in other works (nos 209–12 and 231–2), and may serve for purposes of dating. It is thought to have been part of the household at no. 67 rue de l'Ouest where the artist was living in 1877 (Rivière, followed by Venturi). On the other hand, Cézanne's comings-and-goings are not fully known. It may look like 1877 in style, though other dates have been suggested (Anderson) : 1879–80, when the artist was at Melun in a house similarly furnished ; or 1881 when he was back at a house in rue de l'Ouest, Paris.

209. Plate of Apples
Chicago (Ill.), Art Institute
46 × 55 s *1877* V.120
See no. 208.

210. Apples and Plate of Biscuits
38 × 55 *1877* V.212
See no. 208.

211. Jar, Cup and Fruit
New York, Metropolitan Museum of Art
60 × 73 *1877* V.213
See no. 208.

212. Flask, Glass and Fruit
New York, Solomon R. Guggenheim Museum
46 × 55 *1877* V.214
See no. 208.

Flowers

213. Delft Vase with Dahlias
Paris, Louvre
73 × 54 s 1873–5 V.179
Painted at Auvers in the house of Dr Gachet ; the vase was there in 1936 (Venturi). Also used as a model by Pissarro.

214. Vase of Geraniums and Coreopsis
52 × 39 s 1873–5 V.180

215. Light-Blue Vase
Moscow, Museum of Modern

167

168

169

170

171

172

173

174

175

177

178

179

176

180

181

182

94

183

184

185

186 (plate VII)

187

188

189

190

191

192

193

194

195

196

199

197

198

200

201

202

203

204

205

206

207

208

95

209

210

211

212

Western Art
56 × 46 1873–5 V.182

216. Small Delft Vase
Paris, Louvre
41 × 27 s 1873–5 V.183
The flowers are massed in bright colour tones of red, yellow and black, with a compact look ; the volume aspect is accentuated by the clear ground.
See plate X.

217. Vase on a Floral Cloth
61 × 50 s 1873–7 V.181

218. Vase on a Round Table
49 × 36 1873–7 V.216
Painted in the house of Dr Gachet at Auvers.

219. Two Vases
54 × 44 1873–7 V.217

220. Green Vase
Philadelphia (Pa.), Museum of Art
46 × 34 1873–7 V.218

221. Vase of Petunias
Zurich, Bührle Collection
46 × 55 1875–6 V.198
Duranty remarked on this painting : "Obviously Maillobert [i.e. Cézanne] thought a kilo of green would be greener than a gram" (Dorival).

222. Terracotta Vase
31·5 × 36·5 1875–6 V.199

223. Rococo Vase
Washington, D.C., National Gallery of Art
73 × 58 s *1876* V.222
Inspired by a Second Empire print. The vase is elaborately baroque, as if under the impetus of the flowers.

224. Plate and Decorated Vase
37 × 32 1875–7 V.215

225. Glass Vase
41 × 33 1875–7 V.184

Portraits

Observation of the subject is close but detached, after Impressionism. However, the resemblance draws more from the character of the artist than mere technical skill. The violent

treatment of earlier days is gone: "Cézanne seemed to be revenging himself on a friend for some secret grudge" (Valabrègue). The approach now is calm; it conveys the sitter's attitude. In particular, nos 242–3 have an introspective air and are among the period's leading achievements.

226. Man with Beard (Self-Portrait ?)
48 × 36 s ? V.21
Sometimes considered an early work, because it is rather traditional in style. The artist's son always dated it later. Possibly the piece accepted for the 1882 Salon through Guillemet's good offices (Venturi) and if so, this would account for a style conventionally acceptable.

227. Madame Cézanne
Paris, Louvre
46 × 38 1871–3 V.226

228. Madame Cézanne
55 × 46 1872–7 V.229

229. Madame Cézanne with her Head Inclined
26 × 30 1872–7 V.228
Cézanne made of Hortense a long-suffering model. The group of paintings which feature her comprise some of his best works. A certain "abstract charm" (Venturi) comes from the well-groomed hair, striped bodice and facial oval.

230. Madame Cézanne Leaning on a Table
61 × 50 1873–7 V.278
See plate XI.

231. Madame Cézanne Sewing
58 × 48 *1877* V.291
See no. 208.

232. Madame Cézanne in a Red Armchair
Boston (Mass.), Museum of Fine Arts
72·5 × 56 *1877* V.292
Cézanne's wife was said to be fashion-conscious and a reader of the *Mode Illustrée* (Van Buren). Her dress is in the fashion of 1877, with a straight, uncluttered line. The background hanging, olive yellow and blue-flowered, appears

elsewhere (see no. 208).

233. Girl with her Hair Down
1873–7 V.277

234. Country Girl
48 × 40 1873–7 V.285

235. Louis-Auguste Cézanne
55 × 46 1875–6 V.227

236. Self-Portrait in a Beret
Leningrad, Hermitage
55 × 38 1873–5 V.289

237. Self-Portrait on Rose Background
65 × 54 1873–6 V.286
Described in a Rilke letter to Clara (23 October 1907), in these terms : "It is drawn with a pre-eminently confident hand, round and hard, the forehead all of a piece. It is solid even when dissolving planes and forms de-limit a thousand contours within the face itself, spear-headed by the growth of beard which strand by strand responds to an incredible intensity of touch . . ."

238. Self-Portrait in a Straw Hat
34 × 26 1873–6 V.287

239. Self-Portrait Outdoors
64 × 52 1875–6 V.288

240. Self-Portrait
24 × 18 1875–7 V.280

241. Self-Portrait with Head Covered
Munich, Neue Staatsgalerie
55 × 47 1875–7 V.284

242. Self-Portrait
Washington, D.C., Phillips Collection
61 × 46 *1877* V.290

243. Victor Chocquet
46 × 36 s 1876–7 V.283
Shown at the 1877 Impressionist exhibition. It was controversial and called "Billoir en chocolat" (Billoir was a murderer, much in the papers). See also *Outline biography*, **1875**.

Various compositions

These are more in line with the previous period and the detachment from Romanticism is less in evidence. Many signs of Delacroix's influence (nos 250, 251, 262, 263, 267 and 280). Scenes of agricultural labour tie in with Pissarro (nos 274–5). The subject treatment, is new—in a luminous spatial dimension rendered by shorter brush-strokes and clearer colour.

244. Girl in a White Apron, Seated
16 × 13 1871–2 V.1520 B

245. Venus and Cupid
21 × 21 1870–3 V.124
The background view may be the gulf of Marseilles.

246. Courtesans
17 × 17 1871–2 V.122

247. Female Nude with a Looking-Glass
17 × 22 1872 V.111

248. Woman Suckling a Child
23 × 23 *1872* V.233
This may be the artist's wife and son Paul.

249. Man and Seated Woman Outdoors (Conversation Piece)
45 × 54 1872–3 V.231

250. A Modern Olympia
Paris, Louvre
46 × 55 1872–3 V.225
The theme (previously treated with an analogous composition but differing technical solutions, some years before – see no. 36), is taken from Manet (1863). It is a spirited and ironical composition, baroque in design and emotional in content ; there are reminders of Delacroix

213

214

215

216 (plate X)

217

218

221

219

220

222

223

224

225

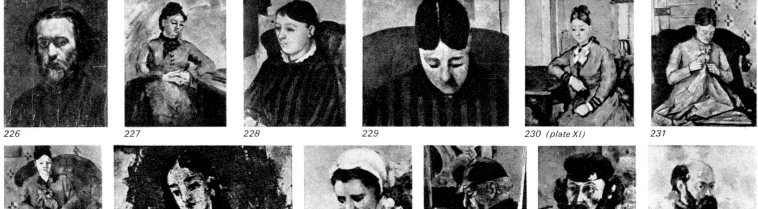

226   227   228   229   230 (plate XI)   231

232   233   234   235   236   237

238   239   240   241   242   243

(Lichtenstein). The pyramidal composition is referable to the same source, also the rich still-life to the left, the sense of colour and the theatrical impetus of the whole. Love, cruelly symbolised by the older painter, turns to idolising on the Baudelaire model. The artist's approach has been described as "romantic still; whereas the technique and visual freedom belong already to the Impressionist school" (Ponente). The beholder in the foreground, against the light, may be Cézanne. See plates IV–V.

251. Afternoon in Naples
30 × 40 1872–5 V.223

A series of oils and water-colours by Cézanne, on the same subject (see also no. 43), may derive from a painting now lost, done in 1863 and turned down for the 1866 Salon (Venturi).

The motif and especially the models and their poses have been identified (Vollard). "The model for this academic piece was a sewage-worker whose wife kept a small dairy. . . . Cézanne asked him to pose which he did, at first under the sheets, in a cotton night-cap – the last touch in the painter's honour. But as there was no point in standing on ceremony with friends, he took off first the night-cap, then the sheets until in the end he posed nude. His wife is in the picture, offering her husband hot wine in a bowl."

Not unlike *A Modern Olympia* (no. 250) in technique; the character of the brushstroke and resplendent palette reflect Impressionism to the full. Mention has been made of Delacroix's influence (Lichtenstein), particularly the *Women of Algiers* at the Louvre, in which similar props were used. But the gestures in Cézanne are not indolent as in Delacroix. They aggressively evoke the erotic concept of the artist, expressed as a personal view.

"How can you like dirty painting!" Thus exclaimed Monet to his friend Guillemet on the subject. But then Guillemet shared the credit with Cézanne for the title (Vollard).

252. Afternoon in Naples
37 × 45 1872–5 V.224

253. Out Fishing
27 × 37 1872–5 V.230

254. A Game of Bowls
17 × 23 1872–5 V.236

255. Drunkards
40 × 50 1872–5 V.235

256. Painter Outdoors
Solothurn, Müller Collection
1872–5 V.237

257. Beside the Seine at Bercy
Hamburg, Kunsthalle
60 × 73 1873–5 V.242

258. "Le déjeuner sur l'herbe"
Paris, Musées Nationaux
(Walter-Guillaume Bequest)
21 × 27·5 1873–5 V.238
See nos 31 and 536.

259. Outing (The Pool)
Boston (Mass.), Museum of Fine Arts
47 × 56 1873–5 V.232

260. Outing
17 × 26 1873–5 V.234

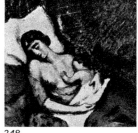

244   245   246   248

247   249   250 (plates IV-V)

97

251

252

253

254

255

256

257

258

259

260

261

262

263

264

265

266

267

268

269

270

271

272

273

275

276

274

277

278

279

280

98

261. Figures Outdoors (Sunday Afternoon ; July Day ; Fishermen)
54 × 81 1873–5 V.243
Shown by Cézanne at the third Impressionist Exhibition (1877), when the theme puzzled Rivière. But the landscape and the attitude of some figures, to the left, may bear comparison with the *Apotheosis of Delacroix* (no. 264).

262. Don Quixote
22·5 × 16·5 1873–5 V.244
As with no. 263, some analogy with *Don Rodrigo*, by Delacroix.

263. Don Quixote
35 × 24 1873–7 V.246

264. The Apotheosis of Delacroix
27 × 35 1873–7 ? V.245
Delacroix is sustained by angels; also, from the right, are represented Pissarro, Monet, Cézanne and his pack, Chocquet and one more figure (unidentified). The dog may stand for envy or critical opinion (Lichtenstein). There is some difference about the dating. The artist wrote to Bernard (12 May 1904) : "I don't know if my poor health will ever let me realise the dream of making his Apotheosis" (understood as that of Delacroix). But an 1874 photograph, published in *Amour de l'Art* (October 1935), shows Cézanne by his easel, and resting on it what looks like a similar painting, perhaps the very same.

265. Tiger
29 × 37 s 1873–7 V.250

266. Female Nude in Bed
8·5 × 13 1873–7 V.279

267. Figures Outdoors (Mythological Scene ; Sancho Panza in the Water)
46 × 55 1873–7 V.239
Some analogy in terms of composition with *Ovid among the Scythians* by Delacroix.

268. The Temptations of St Anthony
47 × 56 1873–7 V.241
The theme was treated on a previous occasion (see no. 29).

269. The Temptations of St Anthony
Parke-Bernet sale 24 May 1968
25 × 33 1873–7 V.240

270. Love Play
42 × 55 1875–6 V.379

271. Love Play
New York, Harriman Collection
38 × 46 1875–6 V.380

272. Labourer Drilling a Well
20 × 15·5 1873–7 V.1520

273. Rural Life
27 × 35 1875–6 V.251

274. Harvest
46 × 55 1875–6 V.249
Gauguin may have owned the painting ; anyhow, he used the motif on a fan (1884) and to decorate ceramics (c. 1886–7).

275. Reapers

25 × 39 1875–8 V.1517

276. Man Putting on a Jacket
Merion (Pa.), Barnes Foundation
31 × 24 s 1875–6 V.248

277. Bathsheba (Susanna Bathing)
London, Korda Collection
31·5 × 23·5 1875–7 V.252

278. Bathsheba
29 × 25 1875–7 V.253

279. Bathsheba
20 × 20 1875–7 V.255

280. The Eternal Feminine (The Golden Calf ; The Triumph of Woman ; "La belle Impéria")
New York, Private collection
43 × 53 1875–7 V.247

Bathers

A "genre" all of its own in Cézanne's painting at this period and even more so later on. The human figures belong to the landscape; the treatment given them, as Venturi observed, like that for water and trees. A crucial stage between representation from reality and pure volume construction, which the artist attained gradually in succeeding periods.

281. Woman Standing
22 × 14 1873–7 V.257

282. Six Women
1873–7 V.265

283. Five Women
50 × 61 1873–7 V.264

284. Woman Sitting
1873–7 V.258

285. Woman Sitting on the Sea-Shore
23·5 × 22 1875–6 V.256
The landscape is of L'Estaque, as again in nos 289 and 290.

286. Four Men
38 × 46 1875–6 V.274
This work and others in the same vein seem to recall the artist's outings in younger days through the Aix countryside (Dorival). Of his companions, Baille and Zola, the latter seems also to have alluded to them in *L'Oeuvre*: "They planned to camp beside the Viosne and live there like savages, in and out of the water all day, needing only a few books for necessities."

287. Four Men
Merion (Pa.), Barnes Foundation
1875–6 V.276

288. Four Men
33 × 41 s 1875–6 V.273

289. Man Standing with Open Arms
23 × 15 1875–6 V.271

290. Man Standing with Open Arms
24 × 16 1875–7 V.259

291. Man Standing with

281 *282* *283*

284 *285* *286*

287 *288* *289*

290 *291* *292* *294*

296 *297*

293 *298* *299*

295 *300* *301*

Open Arms
1875–7 V.262

292. Man Sitting
29 × 21 1875–7 V.260

293. Man Standing with Arms Raised
31 × 21 1875–7 V.263

294. Five Men
24 × 25 1875–7 V.268

295. Man Standing with One Arm Raised
1875–7 V.261
   A drawing was made of this by Paul Signac.

296. Group of Men
19 × 27 1875–7 V.272

297. Group of Men
14 × 19 1875–7 V.275

298. Three Women
22 × 19 1875–7 V.266

299. Three Women
1875–7 V.267

300. Three Women
1875–7 V.269

301. Three Women
Merion (Pa.), Barnes Foundation
35 × 27 1875–7 V.270

The constructive period

1878–87

The Impressionist exhibition of 1877, in which Cézanne took part, was not a success and marks his departure from the group. He wanted his own work to provide motivation and meaning and to rely on his own resources. A letter to Maus of 25 November 1889 explains: "I made up my mind to work in silence until the day I felt able to explain my working results in terms of theory." In fact, the answers he looked for were forthcoming from the actual work process.

Landscapes

As in the Impressionist period, this was Cézanne's favourite line for taking his investigations further. To "construct", he brought form down to essentials: "by way of simplification, Cézanne reaches to the heart of things" (Venturi). A "primitive" time, when the visual reality was opening up before him and he could leave aside, indeed dispense altogether with preconceived intellectual notions. Mindful of Impressionist teaching, he started painting "sur le motif" – outdoors –, studying and recording the subject by exhausting the possibilities under all kinds of conditions.
His landscape output at this period distinguishes the themes, most significantly involved at

subsequent periods in his researches.

302. Pool at Jas de Bouffan
73 × 60 *1878* V.484

303. Viaduct in the Arc Valley
57 × 72 1878–83 V.296

304. Houses and Trees in Provence
Washington, D.C., National Gallery of Art
50 × 61 1878–83 V.297

305. Pilon du Roi
Merion (Pa.), Barnes Foundation 1878–83 V.301
   Upland near Aix.

306. Tree and Dovecot in Provence
Laren, Boerlage Collection
73 × 92 1878–83 V.300

307. L'Estaque from the Sea
Merion (Pa.), Barnes Foundation
44 × 77 1878–83 V.293

308. Lane in L'Estaque
52 × 64 1878–83 V.294

309. Beach in L'Estaque
53·5 × 54·5 1878–83 V.295

310. Provençal Hills with Tree and Houses
Berne, Hahnloser Collection
58 × 79 1878–83 V.302

311. Houses among the Trees
Zurich, Bührle Collection
46 × 55 1878–83 V.305

312. Hills with Trees and Houses
Zurich, Bührle Collection
54 × 73 1878–83 V.306

313. Hills with Fields and

Trees
60 × 73 1878–83 V.303

314. Neighbourhood of Jas de Bouffan
Oslo, Nasjonalgalleriet
60 × 73 1878–83 V.304

315. Médan Castle (The House of Zola)
Glasgow, Art Gallery and Museum
59 × 72 s 1879–81 V.325
   Zola bought a house at Médan in 1878 and Cézanne often went to stay with him, certainly in the summer of 1879 and the spring and summer of 1880, so that this painting can be referable to that time. Originally, it belonged to Gauguin.

316. Trees and Hills
Zurich, Bührle Collection
46 × 55 1879–82 V.299
   Perhaps a view near Aix.

317. Wooded Country and Hills
65 × 81 1879–82 V.298

318. Houses among the Trees
80 × 64 1879–82 V.308

319. Provençal Village
San Francisco (Calif.), Palace of the Legion of Honor (Goetz Bequest)
60 × 73 1879–82 V.307
   Given as northern French countryside (Venturi).

320. Trees and Houses
46 × 55 1879–82 V.309

321. Water-Tank among Trees
Merion (Pa.), Barnes Foundation
1879–82 V.310

322. The Oise Valley

72 × 91 s 1879–82 V.311

323. Hills with Trees and Houses
Stockholm, Nationalmuseum
74 × 93 1879–82 V.317

324. Bridge and Custom House at Pontoise
60 × 73 1879–82 V.316

325. Auvers from Val Harmé
Zurich, Private collection
73 × 92 1879–82 V.318
   The landscape is pin-pointed by the artist's technique of accentuating planes. See plate XVIII.

326. Val Harmé Suburb at Auvers
53 × 85·5 1879–82 V.315

327. Square in a Village
Merion (Pa.), Barnes Foundation
51·5 × 64 1879–82 V.321

328. Fortifications (Gennevillers)
54 × 65 1879–82 V.322

329. Hill with Trees and Houses
45 × 53 s 1879–82 V.323
   It is uncertain whether this is a view of Auvers or Pontoise.

330. Mill on the Couleuve at Pontoise
Berlin, Nationalgalerie
73 × 92 1879–82 V.324

331. Farm-Yard
Paris, Louvre
63 × 52 1879–82 V.326
   Against the bright blue sky, the red roofs and yellow walls of the farm are outlined in light blue. In his search for landscape of a constructive order, Cézanne gave the component elements equal importance; in simplifying, they stand out even

302

303

304

305

307

306

308

309

310

311

312

313

314

315

316

317

318

319

320

321

322

323

324

325 (plate XVIII)

326

327

328

329

330

331 (plate XVII)

332

333

334 (plate XXII)

335

336

337

338

339 (plates XX-XXI)

340

341

343

stronger. See plate XVII.

332. House among Trees
60 × 73 1879–82 V.331

333. Uphill Road
59 × 71 1879–82 V.333

334. Small Bridge (The Bridge at Maincy)
Paris, Louvre
59 × 72 1882–5 V.396
This is one of Cézanne's best-known landscapes. The brushstroke is very regular, the light and shade modulated in passages from green to blue, to yellow. The stress on geometric form has been observed (Venturi).
See plate XXII.

344

345

346

335. Pool at Jas de Bouffan
Buffalo (N.Y.), Albright-Knox Art Gallery
73 × 60 1882–5 V.417

336. House at Jas de Bouffan
59 × 71 1882–5 V.415

337. Houses at L'Estaque
65 × 81 1882–5 V.397

338. Viaduct at L'Estaque
Basle, Kunstmuseum
44 × 53 1882–5 V.401

342

347

348

349

339. Rocks at L'Estaque
São Paulo, Museu de Arte
73 × 91 1882–5 V.404
The landscape rock motif takes the artist's attention at this point, with the focus on dynamic form. See plates XX–XXI.

350

351

352

353

340. Trees and Houses
54 × 65 1882–5 V.403

341. Viaduct at L'Estaque
Helsinki, Ateneumin Taidemuseo
54 × 65 1882–5 V.402

342. Wooded Ravine
Solothurn, Müller Collection
73 × 54 1882–5 V.400

354

355

356

343. Trees and Houses from Above
Basle, Kunstmuseum
60 × 92 1882–5 V.410
A comment from Gasquet. "All self-organised, trees, fields, houses. I see by dabs. The rock-bed, the preparatory drawing, the world above, sinking, bared as if by some catastrophe."

357

358 (plate XXVI)

359

344. Bellevue Houses
Sotheby's sale 4 December 1968
54 × 65 1882–5 V.412
The farm and pigeon-house of Bellevue, near Aix, belonged to Cézanne's brother-in-law Conil. Often a motif of the artist's work.

360

361

362

345. Pilon du Roi from Bellevue
1884–5 V.416

346. Hills with Houses and Trees in Provence
Glasgow, Art Gallery and Museum
49 × 59 1884–5 V.418

347. Countryside with Houses in Winter
1885 V.440

363

364

365

366

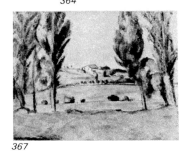

367

368

369

370

371 (plate XXXI)

364. At Jas de Bouffan
74 x 55 1885–7 V.470

365. Jas de Bouffan Neighbourhood
65 x 81 1885–7 V.473

366. Village on a Hill
46 x 55 1885–7 V.482

367. Hill with Trees and a House in Provence
65 x 81 1885–7 V.469

368. Hills with Trees and Houses
63 x 94 1885–7 V.486

369. Trees and Houses
1885–7 V.487

370. Hills and Mountains in Provence (Noon at L'Estaque)
54 x 73 1886–90 V.490
This belonged to Gauguin, who used the subject for a fan dedicated to the Danish painter Peter Krohn. It was sold, probably by Mette Gauguin to Brandes (1891) when Gauguin went off to Tahiti. The mountain country may be L'Estaque.

371. Rocks and Hills in Provence
London, Tate Gallery
65 x 81 1886–90 V.491
As has been observed, the artist lays stress on strength of volume in rocky slopes and the interplay of succeeding planes (Venturi). See plate XXXI.

Trees
A growing interest in trees as a rhythmic element is evident in the paintings of this time.

372. Woodland Scene
55 x 46 1879–82 V.314

373. The Forest of Fontainebleau
63 x 79 1879–82 V.332

374. Fontainebleau under Snow
New York, Meyer Collection
73 x 102 1879–82 V.336

375. Poplars
Paris, Louvre
65 x 80 1879–82 V.335
The vertical element is pronounced and this bears a

348. Médan Village and Castle
(81 x 65) *1885* V.439
In late July 1885, Cézanne was at Médan again, staying with his friend Zola, one of the last, if not the last occasion that he did so before their friendship ended (see *Outline biography*).

349. Mills at Gardanne
Merion (Pa.), Barnes Foundation
65 x 100 1885–6 V.430

350. Gardanne
New York, Brooklyn Museum
92 x 73 1885–6 V.431

351. Gardanne
81 x 65 1885–6 V.432
A colour-fused painting, with no regular brushstroke. It may have inspired the early Cubist landscapes (1908–9) of Braque, Picasso and also

Derain (Richardson).

352. Houses and Trees near Bellevue
Merion (Pa.), Barnes Foundation
81 x 100 1885–7 V.450

353. Fields and Houses near Bellevue
63 x 78 1885–7 V.448

354. Fields and Houses near Bellevue
36 x 50 1885–7 V.449

355. House in Aix Countryside
Merion (Pa.), Barnes Foundation
79 x 85 1885–7 V.451

356. Chestnut-Trees and Farm at Jas de Bouffan
Moscow, Pushkin Museum
73 x 92 1885–7 V.462

357. Chestnut-Trees and Farm at Jas de Bouffan
Providence (R.I.), Rhode Island School of Design
65 x 81 1885–7 V 463

358. House and Farm at Jas de Bouffan
Prague, Národní Galerie
60 x 73 1885–7 V.460
Painting of notable quality, though apparently unfinished. In such instances, the artist's light and colour sensitivity is very patent. The observer gets a keenly accurate impression of the original (Richardson).
See plate XXVI.

359. Farm at Jas de Bouffan
60 x 73 1885–7 V.461

360. Chestnut-Trees and Farm at Jas de Bouffan
31 x 38 s 1885–7 V.465

Vollard says that Cézanne had to "finish" this piece to satisfy an "indiscreet" collector who bought it from the dealer. He did so with reluctance and always regretted it. The treatment of the trees contrasts with the really genuine background (Venturi).

361. Chestnut-Trees and Farm at Jas de Bouffan
51 x 65 s 1885–7 V.464

362. Meadow and Trees at Jas de Bouffan
Ottawa, National Gallery of Canada
65 x 81 1885–7 V.466

363. House with Red Roof
73 x 92 1885–7 V.468
The house has been said to resemble Jas de Bouffan (Venturi), but the lie of the land and the trees look different.

372

373

374

375 (plate XIX)

376

377

378

379

380

381

383

384

382

385

386

387

388

389

390

391

392

393

394

395

396

397

398

399

400

401

402

403

relation to Cézanne's study of tree structure. See plate XIX.

376. At L'Estaque
73 × 92 1882–5 V.409

377. At Jas de Bouffan
60 × 73 1882–5 V.413

378. Near the Exit from Jas de Bouffan
60 × 73 1882–5 V.414

379. Tree-Trunks and Houses (Gnarled Tree)
Arlesheim, Stoll Collection
46 × 55 1882–5 V.420

380. Gnarled Trees
116 × 81 1882–5 V.419

381. Woodland Scene
Cambridge, Fitzwilliam Museum
62·2 × 51·5 1882–5 V.421

382. Woodland Scene
1882–5 V.422

383. Village through the Trees
Bremen, Kunsthalle
65 × 81 *1885* V.438

384. Orchard on a Farm in Normandy
Paris, Ganay Collection
65 × 81 1885–6 V.447
Gowing thinks this is a landscape painted at Pontoise.

385. Orchard
61 × 50 1885–6 V.442

386. Orchard on a Farm in Normandy
London, Aberconway Collection
50 × 65 1885–6 V.443

387. Orchard on a Farm in Normandy
50 × 65 1885–6 V.445

388. Orchard
65 × 50 1885–6 V.444

389. Wood in Provence
Cardiff, National Museum of Wales
77 × 61 1885–6 V.446

390. Countryside at Arc
New York, Suydam Cutting Collection
81 × 65 1885–7 V.472

391. Great Pine and Red Earth
81 × 100 1885–7 V.459
Painted, like no. 392, in the Arc valley.

392. Great Pine and Red Earth
Moscow, Museum of Modern Western Art
73 × 92 1885–7 V.458

393. Chestnut-Trees at Jas de Bouffan
65 × 81 1885–7 V.467

394. Avenue at Jas de Bouffan
73 × 92 1885–7 V.471

395. Big Trees at Jas de Bouffan
London, Home House Trustees
65 × 81 1885–7 V.475

396. Big Trees at Jas de Bouffan
69 × 58 1885–7 V.474

104

404 405 406 407 410

408 409 411 412 413

397. Chestnut-Trees at Jas de Bouffan in Winter
Minneapolis (Mi.), Institute of Arts
73 × 92 s 1885–7 V.476
The subject is a farm-house near Jas de Bouffan, and not the great house as previously thought. In the background is the Montagne Sainte-Victoire.

398. Chestnut-Trees at Jas de Bouffan
65 × 81 1885–7 V.478

399. Houses
Paris, Musées Nationaux (Walter-Guillaume Bequest)
54 × 73 1885–7 V.480

400. Houses
68 × 92 1885–7 V.479

401. Houses
Oslo, Nasjonalgalleriet
60 × 81 1885–7 V.481

402. Viaduct
Moscow, Museum of Modern Western Art
92 × 73 1885–7 V.477
Behind the trees is a glimpse of the Montagne Sainte-Victoire.

403. Mill and Tank
Merion (Pa.), Barnes Foundation
81 × 65 1885–7 V.485
View of the wood of Château-Noir; the subject was studied on more than one occasion, especially in the last years of the artist's life.

Bending road

In the years 1879 to 1882, the motif of the bending road occurred frequently. It goes back, however, to some paintings of about 1870 and the artist returned to it several times later.

404. Road at Auvers from Val Harmé
57 × 72 1879–82 V.313

405. Track in a Wood
55 × 46 1879–82 V.320

406. Côte du Galet at Pontoise
60 × 73 1879–82 V.319
According to Badt, this

painting is of an impression of nature subjected to rigorous order, particularly by means of the vertical stress in the poplars; yet the emphatic bend, known from the Pissarro version of the same subject (1867), is apparently simplified; thus, the S-bend makes a line independent of base directions, embracing the whole field of vision.

407. Wooded Country at Auvers
1879–82 V.312

408. Road with Trees and Pond
81 × 60 1879–82 V.327

409. Village
New York, Wildenstein Collection
54 × 45 1879–82 V.328

410. Hillside Houses
Boston (Mass.), Museum of Fine Arts
59·5 × 72 1879–82 V.329

411. Trees and Houses
60 × 73 1879–82 V.330

412. Trees and Houses
58 × 68 1879–82 V.334

413. At La Roche-Guyon
Northampton (Mass.), Smith College Museum of Art
62 × 75·5 1885 V.441

In the summer of 1885, Cézanne joined Renoir at La Roche-Guyon. It was an unhappy time, for the artist had just been through a brief love affair about which he wrote some letters to Zola.

At L'Estaque (The sea)

The theme of the bay of Marseilles seen from L'Estaque occupied Cézanne's critical attention from 1882 to 1887, the expanses of sea and mountain serving a space-volume function. A different treatment of the theme over the same period is noticeable (nos 307–9)

414. Saint-Henri
66·5 × 83 1882–5 V.398

415. Trees and Houses from Above
65 × 81 1882–5 V.399

416. Trees and Houses from Above
60 × 73 1882–5 V.405

417. View through Trees
London, Butler Collection
73 × 60 1882–5 V.406

418. Marseilles Neighbourhood
60 × 73 1882–5 V.407

419. Mount Marseilleveyre and Maire Island
51 × 62 1882–5 V.408

420. The Gulf of Marseilles
Philadelphia (Pa.), Museum of Art
65 × 81 1882–5 V.411

421. The Gulf of Marseilles
Paris, Louvre
58 × 72 1883–5 V.428

422. The Gulf of Marseilles
New York, Metropolitan Museum of Art
73 × 100 1883–5 V.429
In the distance, the outcrops

414 415 416

417 418 419

420 421 422

423   *424*   *425*

426   *427*   *428*

429. Road at the Foot of the Mountain
Merion (Pa.), Barnes Foundation
45 × 53 1882–5 V.424

430. Upland with Houses and Trees
Moscow, Pushkin Museum
60 × 73 1882–5 V.423

431. View from Gardanne
73 × 92 1885–6 V.434

432. Gardanne Neighbourhood
US Government Property (Charles A. Loeser Bequest)
63 × 91·5 1885–6 V.435

433. Gardanne Neighbourhood
67·5 × 91·5 1885–6 V.437

434. Beaurecueil
Indianapolis (Ind.), Herron Museum of Art
65 × 81 1885–6 V.433

435. Gardanne Neighbourhood
60 × 73 1885–6 V.436

436. Viaduct and Big Trees
New York, Metropolitan Museum of Art

of Marseilles, Notre-Dame de la Garde, Roucas Blanc and Mount Marseilleveyre.

423. Trees and Houses from Above
The Hague, Gemeentemuseum
46 × 55 1883–6 V.427

424. Houses and Chimney-Stack from Above
38 × 46 1883–6 V.426

On the horizon are Mount Marseilleveyre and Maire Island.

425. Houses and Chimney-Stack
73 × 92 1883–6 V.425

426. Mountains
Philadelphia (Pa.) Museum of Art
60 × 73 s 1886–90 V.489

Curious clouds and some parts of the promontory are held to have been added later (Venturi). The stroke appears thick and unaccented in contrast with the light and regular work that characterises the painting. The signature too may have been an addition.

427. Rocks and Trees
78 × 97 1886–90 V.492

428. Gulf of Marseilles
Chicago (Ill.), Art Institute
76 × 97 1886–90 V.493

The Montagne Sainte-Victoire

The mountain was a cherished motif with Cézanne from early days. Gasquet remembered him

429   *430*   *431*   *432*

433   *434*   *435*   *436*

437   *438*   *439*   *440*

441   *442*

exclaiming, "Look at Sainte-Victoire, what a line what a thirst for the sun!

How sad at evening when the load falls down... those blocks were of fire... and fire is in them still." It figures, in the period from 1885 to 1887 *(given various view-points and the play of relief around)*, as the expression of his constructive ideal. *"The motif is arid and this*

65 × 81 1885–7 V.452

437. Viaduct and Big Trees
48 × 59 1885–7 V.453

438. The Great Pine
London, Home House Trustees
67 × 92 s 1885–7 V.454

439. The Great Pine
Washington, D.C., Phillips Collection

60 × 73 1885–7 V.455

440. View from the South-West
54 × 65 1885–7 V.456
Probably painted from the Conil property belonging to Cézanne's brother-in-law.

441. View from the South-West
Merion (Pa.), Barnes Foundation
73 × 92 1885–7 V.457

442. View from the South-West
65 × 92 1886–9 V.488

Still-lifes

Cézanne's brush stroke becomes regular and constructive, consonant with his aim to simplify forms. Objects start having volume, at the same time acquiring structure mainly in chromatic terms. It has been observed that intense colours "model by colouring the object" concerned (Bernard).

Fruit and objects

443. Apples and Cloth
25 × 44 1875–80 V.203

444. Vessels, Fruit and Cloth
Moscow, Museum of Modern Western Art
45 × 57 1879–82 V.337

445. Jug, Fruit and Cloth
Moscow, Museum of Modern Western Art
50 × 61 1879–82 V.338

446. Vessels and Orange
New York, Museum of Modern Art
28 × 34 1879–82 V.340

447. Jug, Fruit, Cloth and Glass
Paris, Musées Nationaux (Walter-Guillaume Bequest)
60 × 73 1879–82 V.356

448. Glass, Cloth and Apples
Basle, Kunstmuseum (Staechelin Bequest)
31·5 × 40 1879–82 V.339

449. Fruit-Bowl, Cloth and Apples
Winterthur, Reinhart Collection
55 × 75 1879–82 V.344
There is a knife in the picture, obliquely-angled, after Manet (see also no. 452).

450. Apples and Plate of Biscuits
Paris, Musées Nationaux (Walter-Guillaume Bequest)
46 × 55 1879–82 V.343

451. Cloth and Apples
50 × 61 1879–82 V.346

452. Fruit-Bowl, Cloth, Glass and Apples
46 × 55 s 1879–82 V.341
The painting appears in the *Portrait of Marie Henry* by Gauguin (Chicago (Ill.), Art Institute) and *Hommage à Cézanne* by Denis (Paris, Musée du Luxembourg).

443

444

445

446

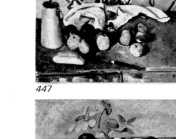
447

448

449

450

451

452

453

454

455

456

458

457

459

460

461

462

463

464

465

466

467

468

469

470

471

472

473

474

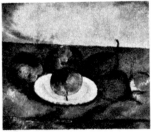

475

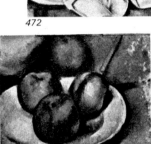

476

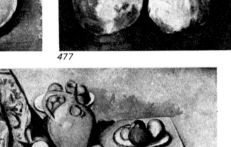

477

478

479

480

481

482

483

484

485

453. Fruit-Bowl, Cloth and Dish of Apples
Copenhagen, Ny Carlsberg Glyptotek
43·5 × 54 1879–82 V.342

454. Plate of Fruit and Jar
Merion (Pa.), Barnes Foundation
18 × 37 1879–82 V.363

455. Plate of Peaches

New York, Solomon R. Guggenheim Museum
60 × 73 1879–82 V.347

456. Plate of Fruit and Sugar-Bowl
24 × 33·5 1879–82 V.1606

457. Plate of Apples, Pears and Grapes
37 × 44 1879–82 V.345

458. Plate of Fruit
Prague, Národní Galerie
19 × 38 1879–82 V.348

459. Plate of Pears and Glass
18 × 38 1879–82 V.351

460. Plate of Fruit
Merion (Pa.), Barnes Foundation
19·5 × 35·5 1879–82 V.352

461. Plate of Pears
1879–82 V.350

462. Plate with Fig and Peaches
28 × 23 1879–82 V.353

463. Plate with Two Apples and a Pear
27 × 35 1879–82 V.354

464. Two Pears, Jar and Knife

New York, Museum of Modern Art
20 × 30 1879–82 V.349

465. Apples
1879–82 V.364

466. Apples
18 × 23 1879–82 V.355

467. Vessels, Cloth and Pot-Plant in Flower

60 × 73 1882-7 V.357

468. Tureen, Bottle and Basket of Apples
Paris, Louvre
65 × 81·5 1883-5 V.494

469. Salad-Bowl, Plate of Apples, Glass and Mirror
33 × 41 1883-5 V.495

470. Vessels, Fruit and Cloth in front of a Chest
Munich, Neue Staatsgalerie
71 × 90 1883-7 V.496
Probably painted, like no. 471, at Jas de Bouffan.

471. Vessels, Fruit and Cloth in front of a Chest
65 × 81 1883-7 V.497
See no. 470.

472. Plate of Cherries and Peaches, Vase and Cloth
Los Angeles (Calif.), County Museum of Art
50 × 61 1883-7 V.498

473. Pot with Lid and Plate of Fruit
35 × 46 1883-7 V.1518

474. Plate of Peaches and Pears
36 × 45 1883-7 V.504

475. Plate of Pears and Apples
36 × 45 1883-7 V.507

476. Plate of Apples
22 × 26 1883-7 V.509

477. Two Apples
14 × 24 1883-7 V.506

478. Two Pears
1883-7 V.505

479. Apples
1883-7 V.508

480. Hanging, Plate with

Jug, Fruit-Bowl and Fruit
43 × 63 1885-7 V.499

481. Jug and Plate with Fruit
43 × 63 1885-7 V.500

482. Two Plates with Big Apples
45 × 59 1885-7 V.502

483. Plate and Two Apples
24 × 33 1885-7 V.503

484. Plate of Apples
38 × 46 1885-7 V.501

485. Plate and Apples on a Cloth
Chicago (Ill.), Art Institute
38 × 46 1886-90 V.510

Flowers

486. Fruit and Vase
Paris, Musées Nationaux (Walter-Guillaume Bequest)
34 × 21 1879-82 V.359

487. Red Vase
40 × 50 1879-82 V.358

488. Vase
46 × 55 1879-82 V.360

489. Light-Blue Vase
41·5 × 22 1879-82 V.361

490. Light-Blue Vase
Paris, Musées Nationaux (Walter-Guillaume Bequest)
29 × 22 1879-82 V.362

491. Green Vase
68 × 57 1883-7 V.511

492. Vase and Two Apples
Zurich, Bührle Collection
55 × 46 1883-7 V.513

493. Vase, Plate, Ink-Well and Fruit (Blue Vase)
Paris, Louvre

486 *487* *488* *489*

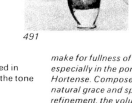
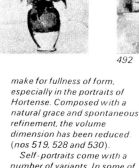

490 *491* *492* *493 (plate XXIII)*

61 × 50 1883-7 V.512
The objects are outlined in blue, and blue is indeed the tone of the whole work. The flower-vase, which had hitherto been considered as an entity of its own now forms part of a more complex composition. See Plate XXIII.

Portraits

Cézanne, having favoured the direct probe of character – and indeed of soul – in the Impressionist period, now changes his attitude. The pace is altogether slower and steadier. His models now seem to be imbued with "straightforward vegetating life" (Raynal). This applies to his young son Paul, his wife and his friend Chocquet. Thin colour impasto and the fusion of the brushstrokes make for fullness of form, especially in the portraits of Hortense. Composed with a natural grace and spontaneous refinement, the volume dimension has been reduced. (nos 519, 528 and 530).

Self-portraits come with a number of variants. In some of them (for example, nos 509-11), the artist has used a more stylised approach, the figure being neatly detached from the ground; he also seems to be conducting something of an objective analysis of himself.

494. Head of a Boy
22 × 16 1877-80 V.281
This has been said to represent the artist's son Paul, aged 7 (Gowing).

495. Head of a Boy
Parke-Bernet sale 26 October 1967

22 × 13 1877-80 V.282
This may, like the previous number, represent the artist's son.

496. Head of Young Paul
29 × 32 1879-82 V.1522

497. Louis Guillaume
Washington, D.C., National Gallery of Art
56 × 47 1879-82 V.374
The model was the son of a neighbour.

498. Madame Cézanne with a Fan
Zurich, Bührle Collection
92·5 × 73 1879-82 V.369
A garment similar to that worn by Hortense Fiquet has been traced (Van Buren) to the *Journal des Dames* of 15 October 1878. See plate XIV.

499. Madame Cézanne in a Garden
Paris, Musées Nationaux (Walter-Guillaume Bequest)
81 × 65 1879-82 V.370
It appears to be a study; part of the background has not been filled in. See plate XV.

500. Woman in a Fur
53 × 49 1879-82 V.376
This seems to have been inspired by a print in the *Magasin pittoresque* of 1860 which in turn, was after an El Greco, the *Lady in Ermine*. But the features may resemble Cézanne's sister Marie. Cézanne must have modelled his work on the magazine, as he had copied Lancret, for the fame of El Greco in France was less in 1880 than subsequently (Badt).
Sterling states that, as the Louvre had nothing of El Greco until just before or immediately upon Cézanne's death, and as Cézanne had never been to Spain, the resemblance might spring from a visual kinship of perception (Sterling).

501. Victor Chocquet
Columbus (Ohio), Gallery of Fine Arts
46 × 38 1879-82 V.373

502. Victor Chocquet
Upperville (Va.), Mellon Collection
35 × 27 1879-82 V.375

494 *495* *496* *497* *498 (plate XIV)*

499 (plate XV) *500* *501* *502* *503 (plate IX)*

504 *505* *506* *507 (plate XVI)* *508*

509

510

511

512

513

515

514

516

517

518

519

520

521

522

523

524 (plate XXIV)

525

526

527

528

529

530

531

532

533

534

painted in 1902, after the subject's death in 1899 and from a photograph.

523. Head of a Boy
28 × 32 1883–7 V.1521
Painted on paper

524. Man Seated
Basle, Kunstmuseum
(Staechelin Bequest)
55 × 46 1883–7 V.1519
See plate XXIV

525. Self-Portrait with a Palette
Zurich, Bührle Collection
92 × 73 1885–7 V.516

526. Jules Peyron
25 × 31 1885–6 V.1607

527. Jules Peyron
46 × 38 1885–7 V.531

528. Madame Cézanne in Half Bust
73 × 60 1885–7 V.529

529. Madame Cézanne
47 × 39 1885–7 V.530

530. Madame Cézanne in a Shawl
Merion (Pa.), Barnes Foundation
89 × 71 1885–7 V.522

531. Madame Cézanne
Ardmore (Pa.), White Collection
46 × 38 1885–7 V.524

532. Madame Cézanne
New York, Solomon R. Guggenheim Museum
50 × 46 1885–7 V.525

533. Madame Cézanne with Clasped Hands
99 × 77 1885–7 V.528

534. Madame Cézanne in a Pleated Bodice
Paris, Musées Nationaux
(Walter-Guillaume Bequest)
81 × 65 1885–90 V.523

Various compositions

Some of the subjects here seem to relate to literature or mythology, some to themes already treated earlier (no. 536 for example). But the real purpose was to work out the figure-space interrelation (see nos 539–40), or problems of structure and rounded forms in the female nude.

535. Female Nude with a Mirror
Merion (Pa.), Barnes Foundation
32 × 25 * 1878 * V.254
This was inspired by a painting of Delacroix, with additional component elements.

536. "Le déjeuner sur l'herbe"
34 × 39 1877 × 82 V.377
The subject was previously treated by the artist (nos 31 and 258). The debt to Manet is now in the title only.

537. Outing by Boat
1879–82 V.378

538. Reclining Boy
Worcester (Mass.), Art Museum
54 × 65 1882–7 V.391

503. Self-Portrait in a Hat
Berne, Kunstmuseum
65 × 51 1879–82 V.366
"Cézanne's geometric analysis is explicit here in the play of angles, triangles and parallels; the face stands out on a cylindriform ground without a hint of dryness because the artist was 'drawing with his brush'" (Raynal). See plate IX.

504. Self-Portrait
London, Tate Gallery
34 × 27 1879–82 V.365

505. Self-Portrait
Winterthur, Reinhart Collection
33 × 24 1879–82 V.367

506. Self-Portrait
Moscow, Museum of Modern Western Art
46 × 38 1879–82 V.368

507. Self-Portrait
Paris, Louvre
26 × 15 1880–1 V.371
This belonged to Pissarro. It has a vigorous approach, showing acute self-observation and at the same time, a determination to abstract and simplify. See plate XVI.

508. Self-Portrait
57 × 47 1880–1 V.372
This portrait was painted on wood and taken from the *Portrait of Cézanne* done in pastels by Renoir (1880), and now in Chicago (Ill.) (Ittleson Collection).

509. Self-Portrait
Paris, Goulandris Collection
25 × 25 1883–5 V.517

510. Self-Portrait
34 × 25 1883–5 V.518

511. Self-Portrait in a Bowler-Hat
Paris, Niarchos Collection
41 × 34 1883–5 V.515

512. Self-Portrait in a Bowler-Hat
Copenhagen, Ny Carlsberg Glyptotek
44·5 × 35·5 1883–7 V.514

513. Paul Cézanne
25 × 20 1883–5 V.534

514. Paul Cézanne
Paris, Musées Nationaux
(Walter-Guillaume Bequest)
35 × 38 1883–5 V.535

515. Paul Cézanne
19·5 × 11·2 1883–5 V.536

516. Paul Cézanne in a Hat
Washington, D.C., National Gallery of Art
65 × 54 1885 V.519

517. Madame Cézanne
20·3 × 15·8 1883–5 V.533

518. Madame Cézanne
Paris, Berggruen Collection
46 × 38 *1885* V.520

519. Madame Cézanne
Philadelphia (Pa.), Museum of Art
46 × 38 *1885* V.521

520. Madame Cézanne
Philadelphia (Pa.), Museum of Art
46 × 38 1883–7 V.526

521. Madame Cézanne with her Hair Down
Philadelphia (Pa.), McIlhenny Collection
62 × 51 1883–7 V.527

522. Victor Chocquet
46 × 38 1883–7 ? V.532
According to Rivière this was

539. Water-Maidens
35 × 44 1883–5 V.538

540. The Judgment of Paris
52 × 62 1883–5 V.537

541. Leda and the Swan
Merion (Pa.), Barnes
Foundation
60 × 73 1886–90 ? V.550
According to Vollard the
inspiration was drawn from
Lady with a Parrot by Courbet

535

536

537

538

539

540

541

542

542. Reclining Female Nude
40 × 55 1886–90 ? V.551
On the left, a still-life painted
with the canvas the other way
round. It is said to be an
illustration of Zola's *Nana*.
(Vollard). But Venturi's thesis is
that the novel was finished in
1880 at Médan, whereas the
style of painting looks later than
that date.

Bathers

*The image construction
relying especially on colour
becomes rhythmical, and this
creates a counter-point between
figures and landscape. The
culmination comes in the next
period, with the "Grandes
baigneuses" (compare nos 543,
562 and 563). The brush-work
is regular and slightly oblique;*
*plastic mass is read from the
foreground to the back and this
adds to dynamic stress to the
composition, more meaningful
in the outcome than the poses
of the various figures.
The Bather Standing (nos
555–6, and 558–60)
represents another theme which
the artist explored several times:
as a study to correlate with
larger and more complex*
*paintings, or else as an essay in
realism. Here, the strength of
composition relies on geometric
structure in terms of horizontal,
perpendicular and oblique lines.*

543. Three Women
Paris, Petit Palais
58 × 54·5 1879–82 V.381
Given to the museum by
Matisse, who bought it in his
youth.

544. Four Women
46 × 38 1879–82 V.384

545. Four Women
27 × 35 1879–82 V.386

546. Five Women
Merion (Pa.), Barnes
Foundation
40 × 42 1879–82 V.383

547. Five Women

543

544

545

546

547

548

549

550

551

552

553

554

555

556

43 × 53 1879–82 V.385

548. Five Women
38 × 41 1879–82 V.382

549. Seven Men
38 × 46 1879–82 V.387

550. Five Men
19 × 26 1879–82 V.388

551. Five Men
35 × 39 1879–82 V.389

557

558

559

560

552. Five Men
60 × 73 1879–82 V.390

553. Two Men
Zurich, Bührle Collection
42·5 × 33 1879–82 V.392

554. Three Men
35 × 22 1879–82 V.395

555. Man Standing, Rear View
33 × 22 1879–82 V.393

556. Man Standing, Rear View
27 × 17 1879–82 V.394

557. Six Men
39 × 53 1883–7 V.541

558. Man Standing, Arms Extended
33 × 24 1883 V.544
In the background is a landscape of L'Estaque as in no. 559.

559. Man Standing, Arms Extended
73 × 60 1885–7 V.549

560. Man Standing, Hands on Hips
New York, Museum of Modern Art
126 × 95 1885–7 V.548

561. Women in Front of a Tent
Stuttgart, Staatsgalerie
63 × 81 1883–5 V.543

562. Eight Women
28 × 44 1883–7 V.540
The stretcher is inscribed, in the hand of Cézanne, with the following words : "Hommage respectueux de l'auteur à la Reine des Félibriges, P. Cézanne 5 Mai 1896."

563. Eight Women
28·5 × 51 1883–7 V.539

564. Five Women
20 × 21 1883–7 V.545

565. Four Women
39 × 35 1883–7 V.547

566. Five Women
Basle, Kunstmuseum
65·5 × 65·5 1885–7 V.542
The composition focuses on the female figures ; now much simplified, they impress one as solemn and monumental.
See plate XXV.

Period of synthesis

1888–1906

Cézanne began seeing less of people. The reasons were various, one being his persistent quest of style control. Living withdrawn, his preference turned more and more in the direction of Aix and the countryside around it, where he made long stays before finally settling down.

Young artists, such as Bernard and Camoin, paid him visits. The critical attention which his work eventually attracted made them want to hear his views and see him at work. But he guarded his solitude, preferring to paint on alone and travel daily to a chosen spot "sur le motif", somewhere outdoors.

The subjects are sometimes new : the *Card-Players* (nos 630–40), or the masked figures (nos 621–4). In the main, his interests continue unchanged, as throughout his working life. The aim was still to perfect and synthesise, and confront the problems inherent in the demands he made of himself.

Portraits

In Cézanne's painting of this period, the function of the model is stressed. Features are carefully delineated, the underlying logic firmly constructive, to the exclusion of pleasing individual facts. As a result, he arrives at a kind of characterisation of a particular type of human being (see nos 567, 574, 599, 601, 610 and most especially no. 612). The form is concise, the geometrics sound; the effect is of a solemn and monumental order (nos 569, 572 and especially no. 578). The attitude is quite natural (nos 579 and 580), achieving a synthesis relative to the figure and the ground. The colour, especially in the later work, of a thinner flowing paste, consonant with the artist's long experience in watercolour technique. Where the action of light governs the material (nos 616 and 620), the figure loses nothing of its solidity.

567. Gardener with a Hoe
Merion (Pa.), Barnes Foundation
64 × 53 1886–90 V.546

568. Victor Chocquet
81 × 65 1889 V.562

569. Madame Cézanne in the Conservatory
New York, Metropolitan Museum of Art
92 × 73 *1890* V.569
One of the best-known portraits of Hortense. A good deal of canvas is left uncovered, but the effect is at once elegant and graceful. "The continuous line of the brow, the facial oval beneath the concave area of hair, the nose, mouth and chin of formal regularity, reveal the artist's geometric ideal" (Venturi).

570. Madame Cézanne in a Yellow Chair
Chicago (Ill.), Art Institute
81 × 65 1890 V.572
The red dress contrasts with the yellow chair ; in the ground are various tones of light-blue. The portrayal of the artist's wife has been described as follows. "The lady's character is clear, calm, satisfied, simple and attractive ; turned forty and very nineteenth-century, she is eminently middle-class" (Venturi).
See plate XLVI.

571. Madame Cézanne in a Yellow Chair

81 × 65 1890–4 V.571

572. Madame Cézanne in Red
São Paulo, Museu de Arte
89 × 70 1890–4 V.573
The simple pose, the crystal clarity of light mould the figure superbly ; the oval rhythm works slowly but overall, gentle yet massive like a new Giotto" (Valsecchi).
In the red-dress portraits of about 1890, the "perspective cube of traditional representation has quite disappeared" (Ponente). The painter in fact "achieves a new synthesis between figure and setting, making the image come across with greater monumentality".
See plate XLI.

573. Madame Cézanne in a Yellow Chair

116 × 89 1890–4 V.570

574. Madame Cézanne in a White Dressing-Jacket
55 × 46 1890–4 V.577

575. Self-Portrait in a Soft Hat
1890–4 V.579

576. Self-Portrait
46 × 40 1890–4 V.578

577. Labourer Seated
55 × 46 1890–4 V.565

578. Woman with a Coffee-Pot
Paris, Louvre
130 × 97 1890–4 ? V.574
According to the artist's son this was painted in 1887. Venturi thinks it is later, and it is dated 1892 by Gowing, and 1890–2 by Cooper. The sitter was a servant at Jas de Bouffan.

562

563

564

561

565

566 *(plate XXV)*

567

568

569

570 *(plate XLVI)*

571

572 *(plate XLI)*

573

574

575

576

577

578 *(plate XXXII)*

See plate XXXII.

579. Boy in a Red Waistcoat, Side View
81 × 65 1890–5 V.680
Traditionally said to represent an Italian boy called Michelangelo Di Rosa.

580. Boy in a Red Waistcoat Leaning on his Elbow
Zurich, Bührle Collection
79·5 × 64 1890–5 V.681
The boy's arm, very long in proportion to the body, expresses a sense of utter relaxation on the part of the model.
See plates XLIX–L.

581. Boy in a Red Waistcoat, Standing
92 × 73 1890–5 V.682

582. Boy in a Red Waistcoat, Front View
Merion (Pa.), Barnes Foundation
65 × 54 1890–5 V.683

583. Girl with a Doll
92 × 73 1892–6 V.675

584. Woman Seated with a Book
Merion (Pa.), Barnes Foundation
92 × 73 1892–6 V.575

585. Bust of Seated Woman
65 × 54 1892–6 V.576

586. Madame Cézanne in a Hat
Merion (Pa.), Barnes Foundation
100 × 81 1894–5 V.704

587. Girl in Half-Bust
55 × 46 1894–5 V.676

588. Bust of a Young Man
73 × 60 1894–5 V.677

589. Gustave Geoffroy
116 × 89 1895 V.692
Painted in the Belleville house, between April and July 1895. See also *Outline biography*, **1894**.

590. Boy with a Skull
Merion (Pa.), Barnes Foundation
130 × 97 1894–6 V.679
There is a Giulio Campagnola engraving, similarly composed. As in Delacroix, death was often present in the work of Cézanne (Lichtenstein). The tragic view of life was part of the Romantic concept of Love.
"It was a canvas that he loved . . . one of the few he sometimes mentioned after the work had been given away" (Gasquet).

591. Boy with a Book
1894–6 V.678
The same young man of no. 590 was the model.

592. Italian Girl Leaning on a Table
New York, Bakwin Collection
92 × 73 *1896* V.701
Probably painted in Montmartre, rue Gabrielle ; the model was a relative of Michelangelo Di Rosa, the *Boy in a Red Waistcoat* (nos 579–82).

593. Girl in a Straw Hat
69 × 58 1896 V.700

594. Girl in a Straw Hat
81 × 65 1896 V.698

595. Joachim Gasquet
Prague, Národní Galerie
65 × 54 1896–7 V.694
Gasquet was a poet from Aix, later among the artist's biographers ; Cézanne met him in 1896. Here, again the element of form is stressed and in consequence the definition of planes and volume content, the whole being achieved by contrasting chromatic values.
See plate LIV.

596. Henri Gasquet
55 × 46 1896–7 V.695
The sitter was the father of Joachim Gasquet.

597. Woman Sitting at a Table
64 × 53 1895–1900 V.1611

598. Man with Folded Arms (The Clockmaker)
New York, Solomon R. Guggenheim Museum
92 × 73 1895–1900 V.689

599. Man with Folded Arms
Annapolis (Ma.), Mitchell Collection
92 × 73 1895–1900 V.685

600. Man with a Pipe, Leaning on a Table
Mannheim, Städtische Kunsthalle
92 × 73 1895–1900 V.684

601. Man with a Pipe, Leaning on a Table
Leningrad, Hermitage
92 × 73 1895–1900 V.686

602. Man with a Pipe Leaning on a Table
Moscow, Museum of Modern Western Art
92 × 73 1895–1900 V.688

603. Drinker
46 × 37 1895–1900 V.690

604. Bust of a Seated Peasant
81 × 65 1895–1900 V.687
On the right is a sketch of female figure.

605. Peasant Seated
1895–1900 V.691

606. Ambroise Vollard
Paris, Petit Palais
100 × 81 1899 V.696
The sitter was a collector, art-dealer and writer. Shortly before 1894, he came and settled in the rue Lafitte, Paris where the galleries were. Rewald writes that "Vollard's taste in matters artistic was not over-confident and at first he was relatively undiscerning. But, knowing his shortcomings, he welcomed advice from other people. By good fortune, it happened to come from Pissarro and sometimes Degas. On this, he was quick to act. At Pissarro's insistence, he got in contact with Cézanne who sent in no less than 150 paintings. This was more than Vollard could exhibit at any one time. The Vollard exhibition opened in the autumn of 1895. Cézanne had not shown in

579   580 (plates XLIX-L)   581   582

583   584   585   586

587   588   589   590

591   592   593   594

595 (plate LIV)   596   597   598

599   600   601   602

603   604   605   606

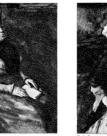

607 608 609 610 611 612 (plates LVII-LVIII) 613

614 615 616 (plate LXIII) 617 618 619 620

Paris for nearly twenty years, so the result was little short of startling. The public as usual took offence, the critics continued to give him bad notices but the artists of the avant-garde and his old colleagues hailed him as a master."

Vollard wrote the first Cézanne biography, richly anecdotal and with a chapter on this very portrait.

607. Man Seated with a Paper
Oslo, Nasjonalgalleriet
100 × 73 1898–1900 V.697

608. Self-Portrait with Beret and Beard
65 × 54 1898–1900 V.693

609. Girl with a Doll
73 × 60 1900–2 V.699

610. Lady in Blue
Moscow, Museum of Modern Western Art
88 × 71 1900–4 V.705
The model is the same as in no. 611.

611. Lady with a Book
65 × 50 1900–4 V.703

612. Old Woman with a Rosary
London, National Gallery
85 × 65 1900–4 V.702
Cézanne spent eighteen months at work on this old lay-sister to whom he habitually gave alms. Gasquet recalled Cézanne having seen "a touch of Flaubert" in the picture, "a mood, something indefinable, a flow of colour red and bluish, which I think belongs to Madame Bovary". See plates LVII and LVIII.

613. Peasant Seated, with a Stick
72 × 58·5 1900–4 V.713

614. Peasant Seated, with a Soft Hat
Ottawa, National Gallery of Canada
92 × 73 1900–4 V.712

615. Peasant Seated Outdoors
65 × 54 1900–6 V.714

616. Vallier Full-Length (The Gardener)

London, Tate Gallery
63 × 52 1900–6 V.715
Vallier the gardener was the model for Cézanne's last portraits. The brushstroke is free and fluid, in token of the ever-increasing mastery of watercolour technique. See plate LXIII.

617. Vallier Full-Length
65 × 54 1904–6 V.1524

618. Beggar (Vallier)
Washington, D.C., National Gallery of Art
107·4 × 74·5 1904–5 V.716
This portrait has been said to result from the following combination: an old beggar, who served as model; and after he left, Cézanne himself – who put on old clothes in order that the work might continue (Gasquet). The resemblance to Vallier, however, is too plain to disregard (Venturi).

619. Beggar (Vallier)
100 × 81 1904–5 V.717

620. Vallier in a Straw Hat
65 × 54 1906 V.718
The paint here is thick and creamy, the brush-work very free. It is deemed Cézanne's final portrait (Venturi).

Various compositions

In this field too, Cézanne's growing preoccupation with the human figure is apparent. A brief series of costumed figures (nos 621–4) belong to a world apart rather than to the realm of humour; their vigour is impressive. Delacroix was still admired by Cézanne; see the copy (no. 629) of one of his works. The Card-Players motif deserves separate mention; it is not wide-ranging in itself, but significant within the limited number of master-themes.

621. Mardi-Gras
Moscow, Museum of Modern Western Art
100 × 81 1888 V.552
The date was supplied by Chocquet, the painting's original owner. According to the artist's son, however, it was done in the Paris studio, rue du Val-de-Grâce. A niece of Cézanne's thought it painted at Jas de Bouffan. The models were: for Harlequin, the painter's son Paul, and for Pierrot, Louis Guillaume. The two figures have also been held to represent Cézanne and Zola (Badt).
The influence of the French

popular theatre has also been suggested (Sterling), because of the set, innocent expressions; a link with the spirit of Le Nain's day and the ingenious gravity of Épinal's colour prints.

622. Harlequin
92 × 65 1888–90 V.553

623. Harlequin
92 × 65 1889–90 V.554

624. Harlequin
1888–90 V.555

625. Preparing a Banquet
45 × 53 *1890* V.586

626. Boat and Bathers
30 × 124 1890–4 V.583
The canvas is now in three pieces, the sides in the Walter-Guillaume Bequest collection, Musées Nationaux, Paris and the centre portion, whereabouts unknown.
It was intended for Chocquet's apartment, like no. 627; probably as an over-door painting. Commissioned in 1888 it was however unfinished by Chocquet's death (1891); it was included in the Chocquet sale of 1899.

627. Fountain (Trough with a Peacock)
30 × 124 1890–4 V.584

On the art market, New York. See no. 626.

628. Female Nude
Geneva, Waechter Collection
93 × 71 *1895* V.710
The model is said to have been one Marie-Louise (G. Rivière); or perhaps the artist's wife (Venturi).

629. Hagar in the Wilderness
50 × 65·5 1899 V.708
Copy of a Delacroix which had belonged to Chocquet; in 1899, Vollard bought it and gave it to Cézanne (Venturi).

Card-players

Painted about 1890–2 at Aix, the subjects were local peasants. Portrait studies (nos 630, 631, 633, 636, 637 and 640) precede the composite work, when each individual assumes universal significance. It is done by conclusive handling of form, synthesised gesture and intense colour areas creating a serried whole. "Zonal rhythm" (Venturi) stands instead of the modelling of form. As Cézanne explained to Larguier, "Painting does not mean making a slavish copy of the object in view; it is capturing the harmony between

621 622 623 624 629

625 626 627 628

variously related things."

630. Peasant Standing with Folded Arms
Merion (Pa.), Barnes Foundation
1888–9 V.561

631. Man with a Pipe and Folded Arms
39 × 30 1890–2 V.563

632. Five Card-Players
Merion (Pa.), Barnes Foundation
134 × 181 1890–2 V.560

633. Card-Player
Worcester (Mass.), Art Museum
32 × 35 1890–2 V.568

634. Four Card-Players
65 × 81 1890–2 V.559

635. Two Card-Players
London, Home House Trustees
58 × 69 1890–2 V.557
The man on the left is the gardener "père Alexandre". Strikingly put together, the elementary colour contrasts are supported by endless gradations. The yellow-brown of the player on the right, the violet blue of the one on the left ; behind, the slate-blue of the landscape background. See plate XXXV.

636. Man with a Pipe
London, Home House Trustees
73 × 60 1890–2 V.564
A study of "père Alexandre" the gardener, see also nos 635, 638–9. The figure is built by means of elementary planes and the arrangement of colours is complex. "A Cézanne peasant is individual in the portrayal and universal in the idea ; monumental without and unshakably convinced within" (Venturi). See plate XXXIV.

637. Man with a Pipe
26 × 20·5 1890–2 V.566

638. Two Card-Players
97 × 130 1890–2 V.556

639. Two Card-Players
Paris, Louvre
45 × 57 1890–2 V.558
The two players of nos 635 and 638 reappear. The treatment of volume and plane is simpler and at the same time stronger ;

630

631

632

634

633

636 (plate XXXIV)

637

640

635 (plate XXXV)

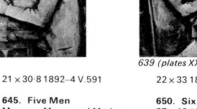
638

639 (plates XXXVI-XXXVII and XXXVIII-XL)

the effect, more life-like still. The landscape background is barely hinted at in tonal values of violet, grey-blue and white. See plates XXXVI–XXXVII, XXXVIII, XXXIX and XL.

640. Peasant
55 × 46 1890–2 V.567

Bathers

Over the previous years, this theme had been given varied treatment. The aim now is to balance landscape with figure content until the latter becomes integral (see no. 657). There are some rather statuesque nudes as earlier. But by degrees, an extraordinary expressive synthesis is achieved (no. 652) and dynamic strength (nos. 653 and 655). The fusion of figures and landscape architecture

results. The colour material is luminous and fluid, light-bluish areas of shade; the line is moist and soft (no. 658). Patiently aligning the means of expression, a consensus is reached embracing all components (of especial significance in this regard is no. 657).

641. Five Men
54 × 65 1888–90 V.582

642. Four Men
Paris, Louvre
22 × 33 1890–4 V.585
See plate XLII.

643. Group of Men and Women
22 × 35 1890–4 V.589

644. Group of Men and Women
Philadelphia (Pa.), Museum of Art

21 × 30·8 1892–4 V.591

645. Five Men
Moscow, Museum of Modern Western Art
27 × 41 1892–4 V.588

646. Four Men
Merion (Pa.), Barnes Foundation
30·5 × 40·5 1892–4 V.590

647. Six Men
52 × 63 1892–4 V.581

648. Group of Men
Paris, Louvre
60 × 81 1892–4 V.580
The attitudes are human, not idealised ; though Cézanne's rounded form makes the nudes lyrical, it remains subordinate to the monumental effect (Raynal). See plate XLIII.

649. Group of Men

22 × 33 1892–4 V.587

650. Six Men
27 × 46 *1895* V.724

651. Group of Men
30 × 44 *1895* V.727
A lithograph of this was made by Roussel, and published in the *Album Cézanne* issued by Bernheim-Jeune, 1914.

652. Group of Men and Women
24 × 27 1900–4 V.728
Published by Venturi when it belonged to Ambroise Vollard, and seen as powerfully expressive.

653. Group of Men
20 × 33 1900–6 V.729

654. Four Women
Copenhagen, Ny Carlsberg Glyptotek

641

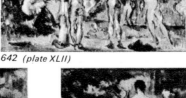
642 (plate XLII)

643

644

645

646

647

648 (plate XLIII)

649

650

651

652

653

654

656

655

657 (plate LV)

660

662

658 (plates LX-LXI)
73 × 92 *1900* V.726

659

661

655. Group of Women
73 × 92 1898–1905 V.725
Probably the preparatory study for no. 657.

656. Four Women
New York, Juviler Collection
33·5 × 20·5 1895–8
Not listed by Venturi; published by Richardson in 1956. It seems directly associable with no. 657, interposing the reclining figure in the group on the right.

657. Group of Women ("Les grandes baigneuses" – I)
Philadelphia (Pa.), Museum of Art
208 × 249 1898–1905 V.719
This "masterpiece of architectonic fantasy" (Venturi) is traditionally said to have taken seven years to paint. A niece of Cézanne's has recently recalled him working it out at the Lauves studio, specially built for him. Certainly it is the most perfectly concluded of the *Bathers* series. All is fused; in the colour atmosphere, relative mass is harmonious everywhere, everything has a place and purpose; its architecture is sublime" (Ponente).
The breathing space between the two groups leads the eye through to a vast landscape

background. This is not distinct from the figures; it includes them, projects them continually back against the distance; the images evoke the landscape and bring it into being (Waldfogel). The arc movement joins the two groups along the line it describes; it also links the various planes and view in the background. Thus, the interval itself which accedes to the background performs a unifying function. See plate LV.

658. Group of Women ("Les grandes baigneuses" – II)
London, National Gallery
130 × 195 1900–5 V.721
Referred to 1904–5 by Gowing, since colour and stroke are directly comparable with his 1905 style. The line is moist and soft, the whole immersed in light-bluish shade; even the usual violet half-tones are muted.
The problem of relating figures and background so that they become integral has been solved even more brilliantly through the medium of a sole reclining figure (Waldfogel): a focus between foreground and background, the first plane of vision and the second, the right-hand and the left-hand group. See plates LX–LXI.

659. Group of Women ("Les grandes baigneuses" – III)
Merion (Pa.), Barnes Foundation
133 × 207 1900–5 V.720

660. Group of Women
Chicago (Ill.), Art Institute
50 × 61 1900–5 V.722

661. Group of Women
29 × 36 1900–5 V.723

662. Sketch with Female Figures
65 × 81 1900–6 V.1523

Landscapes

Nature view, in Cézanne's late period, gain in unity of composition by use of fluid and transparently fused colour. The landscape is at one, whether there is water in it or otherwise. The leafy trees of Chantilly are painted with close criss-crossing brush-work (nos 666–7). The areas of colour are vibrantly luminous throughout. This does not diminish the structural entity; it makes the composition, more synthesised and dynamic (see nos 690, 692, 704 and 730), especially in the case of motifs from the loved Aix countryside of Lauves, Bibémus and Château-Noir.

663. House and Mountain
Zurich, Bührle Collection
73 × 91 1885–95 V.483

664. Avenue at Chantilly
23 × 17 1888 V.626

665. Avenue at Chantilly
Toledo (Ohio), Museum of Art
81 × 65 1888 V.627

666. Avenue at Chantilly
75 × 63 1888 V.628

667. Meadow and Trees
Berlin, Cassirer Collection
71 × 58 *1888* V.633

668. Château de Marines
73 × 92 1888–90 V.636

669. Chestnut Avenue at Jas de Bouffan
81 × 65 1888–90 V.649

670. Pool and Trough at Jas de Bouffan
65 × 81 1888–90 V.648

671. Bellevue House and Dove-Cot
Essen, Museum Folkwang
65 × 81 1888–92 V.651

672. Bellevue House and Dove-Cot
54 × 73 1888–92 V.652

673. Bellevue Dove-Cot
1888–92 V.653

674. Bellevue Dove-Cot
Cleveland (Ohio), Museum of Art
65 × 81 1888–92 V.650

675. Bellevue Dove-Cot
58 × 78 1888–92 V.654

676. "La Colline des Pauvres"
New York, Metropolitan Museum of Art
63 × 81 1888–94 V.660

677. Lines of Apple Trees
Merion (Pa.), Barnes Foundation
1890–4 V.642

678. Provençal House
Merion (Pa.), Barnes Foundation
65 × 81 1890–4 V.643

679. House and Trees
Merion (Pa.), Barnes Foundation
65 × 81 1890–4 V.646

680. Woodland Scene
1890–4 V.645

681. Woodland Scene
1890–4 V.647

682. Bellevue Houses
60 × 73 1890–4 V.655
The planes are clearly defined and the brushstroke moves freely especially in the foliage. See plate XXXIII.

683. Pilon du Roi
Winterthur, Reinhart Collection
80 × 98 1890–4 V.658

684. Hunting Lodge in Provence
Merion (Pa.), Barnes Foundation
54 × 81 1890–4 V.671

685. Trees and Road
73 × 60 1890–4 V.672

686. Ruined House
New York, Haupt Collection
65 × 54 1892–4 V.657

687. Deserted House
49 × 58·5 1892–4 V.659

688. The Great Pine
São Paulo, Museu de Arte
84 × 92 1892–6 V.669
Painted at Montbriant on the property of Cézanne's brother-in-law. See plate XLVII.

689. Clearing
100 × 81 1892–6 V.670

690. Château-Noir
Winterthur, Reinhart Collection
73 × 92 1894–6 V.667
The artist had a studio by Château-Noir, a fine house near Aix. He was often at work there in the late period.

691. Rocks in a Wood
New York, Metropolitan Museum of Art
73 × 93 1894–8 V.673
Perhaps a view of the forest of Fontainebleau (Venturi).

692. Rocks in a Wood
Zurich, Kunsthaus
48·5 × 59·5 1894–8 V.674
Perhaps a view of the forest of Fontainebleau. However, "the actual setting goes for little, given the picture's autonomy. The rebounding perspectives, continually re-aligning, produce a newly-probed depth of emotive content" (Ponente).
Cézanne's words are relevant in this context, as recalled by

663

664

665

666

668

667

669

670

671

672

673

674

675

676

677

678

679

680

681

682 (plate XXXIII)

683

684

685

686

687

688 (plate XLVII)

689

690

691

692 (plate XLVIII)

693

694

695

699

700

701

696

697

698

702

703

704 (plate LVI)

705

706 (plate LIX)

707

709

708

710

711

712

713

714

715

716

717

718

719

720

721

722

723

724

725

726

727

728

Gasquet : "Nature is always the same though nothing remains of what we see now. Art must have impact on nature in recording the elements and appearance that go with each change. Thus, art lets us sample eternal nature." See plate XLVIII.

693. Maison Maria on the Château-Noir Road
65 × 81 1895–8 V.761

694. Big Trees
London, Klessler Collection
81 × 65 1895–8 V.760

695. Woodland Scene
81 × 65 1895–1900 V.1527

696. Woodland Scene
73 × 57 1895–1900 V.1526

697. Montgeroult at Sunset
81 × 65 1899 V.668
Montgeroult was a little village near Pontoise, where Cézanne lived for a while in 1899.

698. Farm at Montgeroult
64 × 52 1899 V.656

699. Rock Cave at Bibémus
Essen, Museum Folkwang
65 × 81 1898–1900 V.767

700. Rock Cave at Bibémus
79 × 63·5 1898–1900 V.772

701. Rock Cave at Bibémus
Merion (Pa.), Barnes Foundation
90 × 71 1898–1900 V.773

702. Mill in Château-Noir Grounds
Philadelphia (Pa.), Museum of Art
73 × 92 1898–1900 V.768
The mill was still on site in 1936.

703. Sea at L'Estaque
97 × 78 1898–1900 V.770

704. Trees and Rocks
New York, Museum of Modern Art
81 × 65 *1900* V.774
The location is the Aix neighbourhood, between Bibémus and Château-Noir (Venturi). The wood in a storm is a landscape motif dear to the artist. Tones of light-blue, violet and orange predominate. See plate LVI.

705. Trees and Rocks
79 × 64 *1900* V.775

706. Trees and Rocks (The Red Rock)
Paris, Musées Nationaux (Walter-Guillaume Bequest)
91 × 66 1900 V.776
To the right is the square orange-red rock, positioned, like the blue-green foliage, against a pale blue sky. The violet shadows and orange-red reflected light from the sun give the picture warmth. See plate LIX

707. Rock Cave at Bibémus
Zurich, Bührle Collection
65 × 54 *1900* V.777

708. Rock Cave at Bibémus
65 × 54 *1900* V.778

709. Bibémus
New York, Solomon R. Guggenheim Museum
71·5 × 90 *1900* V.781

710. Water-Tank in Château-Noir Park
73 × 60 *1900* V.780

711. Château-Noir Park
Paris, Musées Nationaux (Walter-Guillaume Bequest)
92 × 73 *1900* V.779

712. Château-Noir Park
60 × 81 *1900* V.784

713. Château-Noir Park
93 × 74 *1900* V.787

714. Bibémus
44 × 53 1900–2 V.782

715. Rocks and Trees at Bibémus
50 × 61 1900–4 V.785

716. Rocks and Trees at Bibémus
65 × 54 1900–4 V.786

717. Rocks and Trees in Château-Noir Park
92 × 73 1900–4 V.788

718. Village Church
92 × 71 1900–4 V.1531

719. Houses on a Hill
65 × 81 1900–6 V.1528

720. Bending Road
73 × 92 1900–6 V.1532

721. Provence Woodland
1900–6 V.791

722. Trees and Rocks
61 × 50 1900–6 V.792

723. Bending Road in a Wood
81 × 65 1900–6 V.789

724. Bending Road
Munich, Neue Pinakothek
81 × 65 1900–6 V.790

725. Trees and Houses (Landscape in Blue)
Moscow, Museum of Modern Western Art
102 × 83 1900–6 V.793

726. Forest
Ottawa, National Gallery of Canada
80 × 65 1902–4 V.1530

727. Les Lauves
64 × 80 1902–6 V.1610

The district is in the neighbourhood of Aix.

728. Château-Noir
Washington, D.C., National Gallery of Art
73·7 × 96·6 1904 V.796

729. Château-Noir
London, Clark Collection
70 × 82 1904–6 V.797

730. Château-Noir
73 × 92 1904–6 V.795

731. Château-Noir
73 × 92 1904–6 V.794

732. House and Trees ("Le Cabanon de Jourdan")
Milan, Private collection
65 × 81 1906 V.805
The painting is unfinished ; it is Cézanne's last painting in oils. "The representation of the dwelling shows the painter's obsessive geometry at work again, when technically freedom of mastery was being attained. Yet in the surrounding trees, the treatment of form is supremely lyrical : it explodes under the thrust of colour feeling. To his dying day, Cézanne knew a tyranny of conflict between mind and feeling." (Raynal) See plate LXIV.

River and lake-side themes

Interest in such themes became marked about 1880–90. Cézanne's main concern was rendering the reflections "transparent enough and so ordered as to have a volume value too" (Venturi). Subsequently, similar themes came in for fresh treatment; the difference is gradual, tending always to abstract and simplify (nos 745, 747 and 749).

733. Banks of the Marne
50 × 61 *1888* V.629

734. Banks of the Marne
Leningrad, Hermitage
65 × 81 *1888* V.630

735. Houses on the Banks of the Marne (Fishermen)
63 × 79 *1888* V.632

736. Bridge over the Marne at Créteil
Moscow, Pushkin Museum
71 × 90 *1888* V.631
An extraordinary feat according to Venturi. The colours reflected in the water have all been ordered in pictorial terms of pure mass.
"The free brushstrokes, transparent as watercolour, do not follow the form of objects . . . instead they run parallel. The different passages of the painting are fused as a result ; the whole is consonant and evokes a sense of the universal infinite" (Malizkaia). See plate XXVII.

737. House on a River Bank
81 × 65 1888–90 V.635

738. Trees and Houses on a River Bank
73 × 92 1888–90 V.634

739. Trees on a River Bank (Waters and Boughs)
75 × 63 1888–90 V.638

740. Trees and Houses on a River Bank
73 × 92 1888–90 V.637

741. Trees and Houses on a River Bank
65 × 92 1888–90 V.639

742. Aqueduct and Lock
73 × 92 1888–90 V.640

743. Bridge over a Pool
Moscow, Museum of Modern Western Art
64 × 79 1888–90 V.641

744. Trees on a River Bank
50 × 61 1888–94 V.644
The colours are unfamiliar in Cézanne ; therefore deemed (Venturi) a copy of a Romantic School work.

745. Lake Annecy
London, Home House Trustees
64 × 81·3 1896 V.762
A view of Château de Duingt on Lake Annecy, seen from Talloires where Cézanne spent the summer of 1896. The tree-trunk in the foreground sets the rest of the landscape further back ; the transparent air-space is thus fused with the composition's massively solid quality and the unity of vision is complete (Venturi). See plates XLIV–XLV.

746. Torrent in a Wood
Cleveland (Ohio), Museum of Art
60 × 81 1898–1900 V.783

747. Trees and Houses on a River Bank
65 × 81 *1900* V.771

748. Houses on a River Bank
73 × 60 1900–6 V.769

729

730

731

732 (plate LXIV)

733

734

735

736 (plate XXVII)

737

738

739

740

741

742

743

Held to be a landscape in the Paris region (Venturi).

749. Trees on a River Bank
64 × 81 1900–6 V.1533

The Montagne Sainte-Victoire

The mountain motif was a favourite with the artist in his later years. Intense chromatic quality is aligned with the breakdown of space in perspective terms (nos 752 and 753). Tonal values, where most warm, make the view draw nearer; the cold hues of the foreground make it step back (nos 764 and 767). Space is thus taken apart in a way that is entirely original. In the artist's own words, "Everything – in art especially – is theory worked out and applied by contact with nature."

750. View From the South-West, with Trees
54 × 65 1890–4 V.661

751. View From the South-West, with Wooded Hill
65 × 81 1890–4 V.662

752. View From the South-West, with Trees and a House
Moscow, Museum of Modern Western Art
81 × 100 1890–1900 V.663

753. Clearing at the Mountain Foot
72 × 91 1897 V.763
The date has been assigned on the strength of family recollection. The artist left the painting in a Tholonet restaurant, whence his sister Marie later retrieved it.

754. From the South-West
55 × 46 1897 V.764

755. Road in the Valley
78 × 96 1894–1900 V.664

756. From the South-West, with Trees
Cleveland (Ohio), Museum of Art
68 × 90 1894–1900 V.666

757. From the South-West
65 × 81 1894–1900 V.665

758. Château-Noir
Tokyo, Ishibashi Collection
1898–1900 V.765

759. View From Bibémus
Baltimore (Ma.), Museum of Art
65 × 81 1898–1900 V.766

760. View From Les Lauves
Philadelphia (Pa.), Museum of Art

744

745 (plates XLIV-XLV)

746

747

73 × 91 1904–6 V.798

761. Road on the Plain with Houses and Trees
65 × 81 1904–6 V.799

762. Meadow and Trees
Kansas City (Mo.), Rockhill Nelson-Atkins Museum
65 × 81 1904–6 V.800

763. Plain with Houses and Trees
Zurich, Kunsthaus
65 × 81 1904–6 V.801
The artist's affection for this landscape motif can be felt in the skill of the composition where the luminous effects are achieved by leaving the canvas bare in places. See plate LXII.

764. Plain with Houses and Trees

748

Zurich, Bührle Collection
65 × 81 1904–6 V.802

765. Upland with Houses and Trees
55 × 95 1904–6 V.804

766. Road on the Plain with Houses and Trees
Basle, Kunstmuseum
60 × 72 1904–6 V.1529

767. Plain with Houses and Trees
Moscow, Museum of Modern Western Art
60 × 73 1905 V.803
This view of the Montagne Sainte-Victoire was included by Maurice Denis in his portrait of Cézanne, painted in 1905, in which the artist was depicted along with his son Paul and Roussel.

Still-lifes

Cézanne stresses the volume of objects; keenly perceptive of form, he achieves definition by the synthesised and simplificatory handling of outlines (see no. 772). The still-life gains a monumental aspect, partly due to a restive arrangement of elements comprised, reminiscent of the Baroque type (nos 770, 771, 774, 779, 794 and 807). A dynamic whirl of composition results. As Cézanne wrote to Bernard, there is a focal point – be it in an apple or a sphere or a head – where particular light-and-shade effects make the edges of things seem to recede and merge at vanishing-point over the horizon. Each component has been transformed by brilliant colour; the brushstrokes merge (nos

749

796 and 807). The space-volume interrelation is governed by a central urge (nos. 834–5).

Fruit and objects

768. Wine-Jug and Plate with Fruit
49 × 59 1888–90 V.609

769. Wine-Jug and Plate with Fruit
38 × 46 1888–90 V.622

770. Vessels, Basket and Fruit (The Kitchen Table)
Paris (Louvre)
65 × 80 s 1888–90 V.594
The monumental, synthesised character is brought out by the complex receding planes of vision. See plates XXVIII–XXIX and XXX.

771. Sugar-Bowl, Jug and

750

751

752

753

755

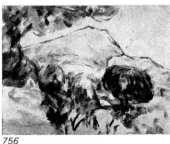

756

  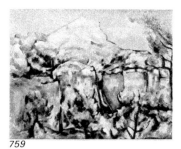

754 757 758 759

760 761 762 763 (plate LXII)

  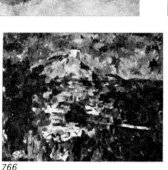 

764 765 766 767

Plate of Fruit
Moscow, Museum of Modern Western Art
61 × 90 1888–90 V.619

772. Jug and Plate with Fruit
Oslo, Nasjonalgalleriet
73 × 60 1888–90 V.593

773. Fruit, Plate and Bottle (The Liqueur Bottle)

New York, Museum of Modern Art
60 × 73 1888–90 V.606

774. Curtain, Fruit-Bowl, Carafe and Fruit
Merion (Pa.), Barnes Foundation
73 × 92 1890–1 V.592

775. Curtain, Wine-Jug, Fruit-Bowl and Fruit

Merion (Pa.), Barnes Foundation
58 × 71 1890–4 V.601

776. Plate of Fruit and Wine-Jug on a Cover
Boston (Mass.), Museum of Fine Arts
32·5 × 41 1890–4 V.612

777. Plate of Peaches and Cover

Winterthur, Reinhart Collection
31 × 40 1890–4 V.607

778. Plate of Fruit and Bottles
50·5 × 52·5 1890–4 V.604

779. Basket with Apples, Bottle, Biscuits and Fruit
Chicago (Ill.), Art Institute
65 × 81 s 1890–4 V.600

780. Bottle and Fruit
Merion (Pa.), Barnes Foundation
50 × 73 1890–4 V.605

781. Vessels, Fruit and Cover (The Peppermint Bottle)
Washington, D.C., National Gallery of Art
65 × 81 1890–4 V.625

768 769 770 (plates XXVIII-XXIX and XXX) 771

772 773 774 775

776 777 778 779

780

781

782

783

784

785

786

787

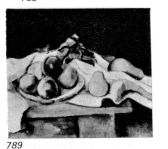

788

789

790

791

792

793

794

795 (plates LII-LIII)

796

797

798

799

800

801

802

803

804

805

806

807 (plate LI)

808

809

810

811

812

813

814

815

782. Apples and Cover
Merion (Pa.), Barnes Foundation
45 × 54 1890–4 V.611

783. Cover, Sugar-Bowl and Plate with Fruit
Philadelphia (Pa.), McIlhenny Collection
51 × 62 1890–4 V.624

784. Straw-Cased Jar and Plate with Fruit
33 × 46 1890–4 V.595

785. Straw-Cased Jar and Plate with Melons
44 × 61 1890–4 V.596

786. Jug and Fruit
The Hague, Gemeentemuseum
50 × 61 1890–4 V.615

787. Fruit on a Cloth
Tokyo, Ishibashi Collection
1890–4 V.603

788. Plate with Apples and Cup (Big Apples)
46 × 55 s 1890–4 V.621

789. Plate with Fruit
1890–4 V.608

790. Plate of Peaches
Merion (Pa.), Barnes Foundation
23 × 35 1890–4 V.614

791. Straw-Cased Jar, Sugar-Bowl and Plate with Apples
Paris, Musées Nationaux (Walter-Guillaume Bequest)
35 × 45 1890–4 V.616

792. Vessels and Plate with Fruit on a Cover
1890–4 V.598

793. Cover, Vessels, Plate with Fruit and Aubergines
73 × 92 1890–4 V.597

794. Curtain, Carafe and Plates with Fruit
Leningrad, Hermitage
54 × 73 1895 V.731

795. Curtain, Fruit-Bowl, Carafe and Plate with Fruit
Paris, Louvre
73 × 92 1895–1900 V.732
"The naturalistic motif is here completely transcended; the artist's vision is affirmed, autonomous, with all the means at his disposal. There are

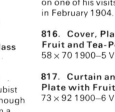

816

several perspective view-points, differentiated so as to emphasise object structure in terms of volume" (Ponente). See plates LII–LIII.

796. Curtain, Vessels and Fruit
New York, Museum of Modern Art
68 × 92 1895–1900 V.736

797. Curtain, Carafe and Plate with Fruit
Merion (Pa.), Barnes Foundation
65 × 81 1895–1900 V.745

798. Straw-Cased Jar and Fruit
Merion (Pa.), Barnes Foundation
71 × 42 *1895* V.737

799. Plate of Fruit, Sugar-Bowl and Straw-Cased Jar on a Cover
New York, Museum of Modern Art
60 × 73 1895–1900 V.738

800. Plate with Pears
The Hague, Gemeentemuseum
38 × 46 1895–1900 V.744

801. Plate with Peaches
The Hague, Gemeentemuseum
36 × 46 1895–1900 V.743

802. Plate with Fruit (Big Pear)

817

818

Merion (Pa.), Barnes Foundation
46 × 55 1895–1900 V.740

803. Wine-Jug and Plate with Fruit
London, Tate Gallery (Stoop Bequest)
53 × 71 1895–1900 V.749

804. Tilted Plate with Fruit
Merion (Pa.), Barnes Foundation
46 × 55 1895–1900 V.746

805. Books, Straw-Cased Jar and Fruit
46 × 55 1895–1900 V.733

806. Skull and Fruit
Merion (Pa.), Barnes Foundation
54 × 65 1895–1900 V.758

807. Onions, Bottle, Glass and Plate
Paris, Louvre
66 × 81 1895–1900 V.730
A clear presage of the Cubist approach (Raynal), even though the artist sets the objects on a uniform ground. See plate LI.

808. Jug and Plate with Fruit
1895–1900 V.750

809. Jug, Glass and Plate with Fruit
55 × 46 1895–1900 V.735

810. Woman and Table with Fruit, Glass and Water-Jar
60 × 73 *1900* V.739

811. Curtain
1900 V.747

812. Skull
1900 V.751

813. Three Skulls
34 × 60 *1900* V.1567

814. Pyramid of Skulls
1900 V.753

815. Three Skulls on Oriental Covering
54 × 65 1904 V.759
Seen in Aix by Émile Bernard, on one of his visits to Cézanne in February 1904.

816. Cover, Plate with Fruit and Tea-Pot
58 × 70 1900–5 V.734

817. Curtain and Tilted Plate with Fruit
73 × 92 1900–6 V.741

818. Curtain, Tilted Plate with Fruit, Carafe and Glass
Winterthur, Reinhart Collection
73 × 100 1900–6 V.742

Flowers

819. Fruit and Vase
Berlin, Nationalgalerie

65 × 81 1888–90 V.610

820. Earthenware Pots
Merion (Pa.), Barnes Foundation
1888–90 V.602

821. Plate with Fruit and Earthenware Pot
London, Home House Trustees
46 × 55 1890–4 V.623

822. Fruit and Pot of Geraniums
73 × 92 1890–4 V.599

823. Fruit and Foliage
29 × 29 1890–4 V.613
This work belonged to Matisse and he made a lithograph of it.

824. Vase of Tulips and Fruit
Chicago (Ill.), Art Institute
60 × 42 1890–4 V.617

825. Vase of Tulips and Fruit
72·5 × 42 1890–4 V.618
Painted on wood.

826. Mass of Flowers
81 × 100 1890–4 V.620

827. Vase in a Garden
65 × 54 1895–1900 V.756

828. Flowers and Greenery
Moscow, Museum of Modern Western Art

819

820

821

822

823

824

825

826

827

828

829

830

831

832

77 × 64 *1900* V.754
Copy of a Delacroix
watercolour.

829. Decorated Vase
Merion (Pa.), Barnes
Foundation
67 × 55 1900 V.755

830. White Vase
40·5 × 29·5 1900–6 V.752

831. Light-Blue Vase
V.748

832. Two-Handled Vase
Washington, D.C., National
Gallery of Art
101·2 × 82·2 1902–3 V.757
Mentioned by Cézanne in

two letters, dated 2 April 1902
and 9 January 1903, both to
Vollard who published them.

Plaster Casts

**833. "Anatomy" by
Michelangelo**
35 × 16·5 *1895* V.709
A lost sculpture, attributed to
Michelangelo and much in
vogue during last century.
Cézanne owned a plaster-cast of
it, which served as a model not
only in the present instance but

as a detail in composition no.
834. Cézanne's treatment of the
cast is stylised in the El Greco
manner (Venturi).

**834. Plaster Cupid and the
"Anatomy"**
London, Home House Trustees
71 × 57 *1895* V.706
On the right is the lower part
of the *Anatomy* (see no. 833).
The plaster statuette is a copy
from Puget. It was remembered
in Cézanne's studio by Vollard
and Denis. Puget was greatly
admired by Cézanne and
Delacroix. Delacroix wrote an
article, also a letter about his
work, praising its strength and

vigour. These were the very
qualities to recommend it to the
painter of Aix.

835. Plaster Cupid
Stockholm, Nationalmuseum
63 × 81 1895 V.707

836. Plaster Cupid
57 × 27 1895 V.711

837. Plaster Cupid
47 × 31 1895–1900 V.1608

838. Plaster Cupid
45 × 30 1895–1900 V.1609

833

834

835

836

837

838

Table of concordance

The corresponding numbers are given here in tabular form, as between the Cézanne paintings (oils only) in the present volume (CWA) and the standard authority (V.): Lionello Venturi, Cézanne, son art, son oeuvre (Paris, 1936).

CWA	V.	CWA	V.	CWA	V.	CWA	V.	CWA	V.	CWA	V.	CWA	V.	CWA	V.	CWA	V.	CWA	V.
1	1–3	85	28	169	167	253	230	337	397	421	428	505	367	589	692	673	653	757	665
2	8	86	29	170	166	254	236	338	401	422	429	506	368	590	679	674	650	758	765
3	10	87	31	171	175	255	235	339	404	423	427	507	371	591	678	675	654	759	766
4	11	88	32	172	168	256	237	340	403	424	426	508	372	592	701	676	660	760	798
5	9	89	27	173	172	257	242	341	402	425	425	509	517	593	700	677	642	761	799
6	4	90	30	174	169	258	238	342	400	426	489	510	518	594	698	678	643	762	800
7	5	91	1510	175	171	259	232	343	410	427	492	511	515	595	694	679	646	763	801
8	6	92	33	176	173	260	234	344	412	428	493	512	514	596	695	680	645	764	802
9	7	93	34	177	174	261	243	345	416	429	424	513	534	597	1611	681	647	765	804
10	16	94	35	178	176	262	244	346	418	430	423	514	535	598	689	682	655	766	1529
11	13	95	37	179	177	263	246	347	440	431	434	515	536	599	685	683	658	767	803
12	14	96	36	180	178	264	245	348	439	432	435	516	519	600	684	684	671	768	609
13	15	97	38	181	170	265	250	349	430	433	437	517	533	601	686	685	672	769	622
14	24	98	46	182	1515	266	279	350	431	434	433	518	520	602	688	686	657	770	594
15	83	99	1512	183	185	267	239	351	432	435	436	519	521	603	690	687	659	771	619
16	87	100	41	184	194	268	241	352	450	436	452	520	526	604	687	688	669	772	593
17	84	101	49	185	189	269	240	353	448	437	453	521	527	605	691	689	670	773	606
18	86	102	43	186	186	270	379	354	449	438	454	522	532	606	696	690	667	774	592
19	100	103	45	187	187	271	380	355	451	439	455	523	1521	607	697	691	673	775	601
20	92	104	44	188	188	272	1520	356	462	440	456	524	1519	608	693	692	674	776	612
21	93	105	53	189	190	273	251	357	463	441	457	525	516	609	699	693	761	777	607
22	94	106	42	190	191	274	249	358	460	442	488	526	1607	610	705	694	760	778	604
23	64	107	54	191	195	275	1517	359	461	443	203	527	531	611	703	695	1527	779	600
24	96	108	39	192	211	276	248	360	465	444	337	528	529	612	702	696	1526	780	605
25	101	109	40	193	192	277	252	361	464	445	338	529	530	613	713	697	668	781	625
26	105	110	47	194	193	278	253	362	466	446	340	530	522	614	712	698	656	782	611
27	115	111	51	195	196	279	255	363	468	447	356	531	524	615	714	699	767	783	624
28	121	112	55	196	197	280	247	364	470	448	339	532	525	616	715	700	772	784	595
29	103	113	57	197	221	281	257	365	473	449	344	533	528	617	1524	701	773	785	596
30	116	114	58	198	219	282	265	366	482	450	343	534	523	618	716	702	768	786	615
31	107	115	50	199	220	283	264	367	469	451	346	535	254	619	717	703	770	787	603
32	117	116	52	200	202	284	258	368	486	452	341	536	377	620	718	704	774	788	621
33	118	117	56	201	201	285	256	369	487	453	342	537	378	621	552	705	775	789	608
34	108	118	12	202	204	286	274	370	490	454	363	538	391	622	533	706	776	790	614
35	104	119	59	203	205	287	276	371	491	455	347	539	538	623	554	707	777	791	616
36	106	120	60	204	206	288	273	372	314	456	1606	540	537	624	555	708	778	792	598
37	119	121	63	205	208	289	271	373	332	457	345	541	550	625	586	709	781	793	597
38	113	122	68	206	207	290	259	374	336	458	348	542	551	626	583	710	780	794	731
39	114	123	61	207	200	291	262	375	335	459	351	543	381	627	584	711	779	795	732
40	90	124	62	208	209	292	260	376	409	460	352	544	384	628	710	712	784	796	736
41	120	125	65	209	210	293	263	377	413	461	350	545	386	629	708	713	787	797	745
42	1520	126	69	210	212	294	268	378	414	462	353	546	383	630	561	714	782	798	737
43	112	127	66	211	213	295	261	379	420	463	354	547	385	631	563	715	785	799	738
44	123	128	67	212	214	296	272	380	419	464	349	548	382	632	560	716	786	800	744
45	125	129	70	213	179	297	275	381	421	465	364	549	387	633	568	717	788	801	743
46	—	130	71	214	180	298	266	382	422	466	355	550	388	634	559	718	1531	802	740
47	18	131	48	215	182	299	267	383	438	467	357	551	389	635	557	719	1528	803	749
48	25	132	136	216	183	300	269	384	447	468	494	552	390	636	564	720	1532	804	746
49	20	133	1513	217	181	301	270	385	442	469	495	553	392	637	566	721	791	805	733
50	19	134	153	218	216	302	484	386	443	470	496	554	395	638	556	722	792	806	758
51	17	135	1511	219	217	303	296	387	445	471	497	555	396	639	558	723	789	807	730
52	1509	136	133	220	218	304	297	388	444	472	498	556	394	640	567	724	790	808	750
53	22	137	155	221	198	305	301	389	446	473	1518	557	541	641	582	725	793	809	735
54	95	138	135	222	199	306	300	390	472	474	504	558	544	642	585	726	1530	810	739
55	75	139	134	223	222	307	293	391	459	475	507	559	549	643	589	727	1610	811	747
56	73	140	137	224	215	308	294	392	458	476	509	560	548	644	588	728	796	812	751
57	80	141	142	225	184	309	295	393	467	477	506	561	543	645	591	729	797	813	1567
58	82	142	138	226	21	310	302	394	471	478	505	562	540	646	590	730	795	814	753
59	74	143	139	227	226	311	305	395	475	479	508	563	539	647	587	731	794	815	759
60	79	144	144	228	229	312	306	396	474	480	499	564	545	648	581	732	805	816	734
61	76	145	145	229	228	313	303	397	476	481	500	565	547	649	580	733	629	817	741
62	77	146	146	230	278	314	304	398	478	482	502	566	542	650	724	734	630	818	742
63	72	147	156	231	291	315	325	399	480	483	503	567	546	651	727	735	632	819	610
64	81	148	157	232	292	316	299	400	479	484	501	568	562	652	728	736	631	820	602
65	126	149	147	233	277	317	298	401	481	485	510	569	569	653	729	737	635	821	623
66	102	150	140	234	285	318	308	402	477	486	359	570	572	654	726	738	634	822	599
67	91	151	141	235	227	319	307	403	485	487	358	571	571	655	725	739	638	823	613
68	99	152	143	236	289	320	309	404	313	488	360	572	573	656	—	740	637	824	617
69	98	153	148	237	286	321	310	405	320	489	361	573	570	657	719	741	639	825	618
70	23	154	149	238	287	322	311	406	319	490	362	574	577	658	721	742	640	826	620
71	85	155	150	239	288	323	317	407	312	491	511	575	579	659	720	743	641	827	756
72	88	156	151	240	280	324	316	408	327	492	513	576	578	660	722	744	644	828	754
73	78	157	152	241	284	325	318	409	328	493	512	577	565	661	723	745	762	829	755
74	89	158	154	242	290	326	315	410	329	494	281	578	574	662	1523	746	783	830	752
75	110	159	158	243	283	327	321	411	330	495	282	579	680	663	483	747	771	831	748
76	109	160	163	244	1520	328	322	412	334	496	1522	580	681	664	626	748	769	832	757
77	97	161	165	245	124	329	323	413	441	497	374	581	682	665	627	749	1533	833	709
78	127	162	1525	246	122	330	324	414	398	498	369	582	683	666	628	750	661	834	706
79	128	163	169	247	111	331	326	415	399	499	370	583	675	667	633	751	662	835	707
80	131	164	1516	248	233	332	331	416	405	500	376	584	575	668	636	752	663	836	711
81	130	165	161	249	231	333	333	417	406	501	373	585	576	669	649	753	763	837	1608
82	132	166	162	250	225	334	396	418	407	502	375	586	704	670	648	754	764	838	1609
83	129	167	160	251	223	335	417	419	408	503	366	587	676	671	651	755	664		
84	26	168	164	252	224	336	415	420	411	504	365	588	677	672	652	756	666		

Index of subjects and titles

Topographical index

*Works not cited in the present index
may be regarded as whereabouts
unknown.*